ALL
ABOUT
NUMBERS

ALSO BY JESSE KALSI

The Power of Home Numbers

ALL ABOUT NUMBERS

Attract Luck, Abundance, and Joy Based on Your Numbers

JESSE KALSI

Waterside Productions
Cardiff-by-the-Sea, California

Printed in the United States of America

First Printing, 2021

ISBN-13: 978-1-954968-27-1 print edition
ISBN-13: 978-1-954968-28-8 ebook edition

Waterside Productions
2055 Oxford Ave
Cardiff, CA 92007

www.waterside.com

Note: Jesse Kalsi has registered the Trademark/Service Mark phrase "number patching" for commercial purposes. All others are prohibited from using the phrase commercially to market business or financial consulting services. The Chaldean code was used to calculate numbers throughout this book. Jesse encourages readers to research all methods of numerology to see which resonates best with them.

Cover Design: Art Direction by Christy Salinas, cover design by Howie Severson
Author Photo by Ben Krantz

This book is dedicated to my ancestors, who fill me with timeless wisdom each day.

CONTENTS

INTRODUCTION

My first book, *The Power of Home Numbers*, was published in 2007 soon after the birth of my son. It evolved into a second and third edition and kept me busy with clients calling me from all over the world. I started a YouTube channel in the same year as the book was released that helped spread my message to like-minded people all over the globe. At the same time, I also had to confront many personal challenges in the years that followed. While I don't like to talk about them, facing and overcoming difficulties has made me a stronger and better person. I have learned a lot from my clients and the suggestions made by many of them have been implemented in this book to better serve the reader.

Other than home numbers discussed in my first book, the influence of numbers can be seen in many aspects of our lives. I have tried to explain the energy of numbers in different areas of our lives based on my experience consulting with tens of thousands of clients of different ages, races, and backgrounds and their complex questions and problems which I had to solve based on my knowledge. I am grateful to God and the Universe for trusting me to work with so many people and being able to serve them.

Intuition and Numbers

I believe in and have experienced the inner calling known as intuition, the inner voice that guides us. I have also realized that most people do not care about it. Numbers have always fascinated me and I continuously observe them to learn more to improve my life. Looking back on my past, I realize how lucky I am to be alive today to write this book. The huge leap of faith that I took to come to the United States has a lot to do with my intuition. Finding my way in a new country and my new home, the United States of America, also has a lot to do with my intuition. My intuition led me to the right numbers that always worked in my favor. My intuition saved me from some close encounters during my days as a flight instructor and in my younger years serving in the Indian Army. It comes strongly and does not go away until I obey the orders being served by the Universe.

As I worked on this book, a thought kept coming to mind. The universe kept instructing me to call a friend whom I have known for many years and who's a best-selling author. Soon after that call, I was at peace: the right publisher had appeared.

My first book has been read widely and many people have called me to teach them what I know. I guess they are being guided by their intuition, as I am by mine. I can see that many people are very confused. In today's world, nobody cares how one is doing and one has to find his or her own way out of challenging situations and improve his or her life. This is why it's so important to use your intuition to guide you to find the right numbers that will change your life.

Sometimes, things start working for you in your home or business while other areas of life don't make any progress. I've met countless people who have wasted time trying to copy other people. We are all different and have different numbers that work for us; no two people have the same set of numbers that benefit them. Once you find your numbers, use them and stick with them until the end to live your best life. You will be glad you did.

CHAPTER ONE

HOW NUMBERS BRING LUCK

How to Calculate Personal Names

Name numerology is very important to attract success in the outside world and fulfillment in our personal lives. The saying "a name sells" is true in the modern world. Our name vibration includes our given name and the way we spell it. This should match our personal energy that comes from our date of birth and harmonize with numbers that bring us abundance and prosperity. As I consulted with clients over the years, I had the chance to balance their names with their dates of birth to attract success. I have many clients who suddenly became lucky after a name change. Most of the people that I consulted with for name changes are regular people and many of them work in the field of media and business. Name changes should be done very carefully by changing or adding one or more letters without altering the actual pronunciation of the name. The way the nickname of the person is written is also important, as that name vibrates in the universe with equal force.

I remember meeting a popular Hollywood actress at an event in Los Angeles. She was a beautiful Canadian lady who happened to live very close to the famous Hollywood sign. She approached me herself and said she had read my book. She started talking about numbers and her life. She had heard about numerology but didn't know how to apply it enough to improve her life. I was glad to show her. After checking her date of birth, I asked her to use a certain middle initial in her name, which she started to do. I was happy to see how her life changed in a few months after our meeting and the name correction. She overcame her financial challenges and got married to a successful businessman. The marriage was solemnized in a cottage once owned by Princess Diana and ever since then, she's been lucky and happy, working on many projects and living the life of the rich and the famous. We are friends and she keeps in touch.

Around the same time, I was contacted by a young East Indian lady who wanted to try her luck in the entertainment business in Bollywood in India. She agreed to make the name change I suggested and we finished our consultation. I didn't hear from her for a while. Sometime later, I was flipping through the pages of a local Indian newspaper that has a big circulation in the San Francisco Bay area. My eyes suddenly landed on a picture of her next to an article highlighting her achievement for being part of a famous soap opera with a top Bollywood Actor. I was happy for her and she did mention in the article that she changed her name to suit her new role.

I can happily say that many of my clients have experienced huge shifts in their lives. I remain ever grateful to the Universe for giving me many opportunities to work with media outlets, companies in Silicon Valley and beyond, and regular people just trying to live more vibrant and fulfilling lives.

There are many schools of thought that associate numbers and letters. I prefer using the Chaldean code, which I find to be more accurate than others. This method is widely used throughout the Indian continent. Let's go through a few examples of personal numerology using the Chaldean code:

Elon Musk, the CEO of Tesla, was born on June 28, 1971.

E L O N		M U S K	
5+3+7+5		4+6+3+2	
20	+	15	=35
Date of Birth:		6+28+1971	=52

Elon has eight letters in his name and the name vibration is also reduced to 35, or 8, much like the energy of the name Facebook. The name energy of Facebook also has eight letters in its name and has similar 35/8 energy. Both are global names.

Being a water sign, Elon's energy works well with the number 7. Cancer is ruled by the number 2 that represents Moon energy. His company name, Tesla, also carries the energy of Neptune that is in sync with his date of birth and the number 28, the day he was born. By looking at his numbers, Elon is highly intuitive and is guided by higher energies. However, he needs to be cautious about his health and not having accidents after his birthday in June 2020.

Donald Trump, the 45th President of the United States, was born on June 14, 1946. He was born under the sign Gemini which is ruled by the planet Mercury and represented by the number 5. In this analysis, we will look at his given name, as that energy vibrates more powerfully:

D O N A L D		T R U M P	
4+7+5+1+3+4		4+2+6+4+8	
24	+	24	=48

Mr. Trump's name carries the energy of planet Venus twice and compounds to planet Jupiter, the largest planet and the giver of good luck and expansion. Venus relates to money, beauty, entertainment, the hotel industry, and the media. Former President

Trump has a set of powerful numbers that puts luck on his side. The number 45 is complemented by Venus and Jupiter energies.

Both the above examples are people born in the month of June but under different sun signs. When calculating names, the date of birth also has to be taken into consideration. The name vibration must match the planetary vibrations so that they flow with the date of birth. The ruling planet of the zodiac sign, along with the total compound numbers, should also be considered.

Sushant Singh Rajput was a famous young Bollywood actor who was found dead in his apartment in a posh Mumbai suburb in June of 2020. The cause of his death is still being investigated and his fans worldwide are interested to know the truth. This matter is also about the justice system in India and whether or not it works differently for the rich upper class than it does for the less privileged in the country. Let's see what we can uncover from his numerology:

S U S H A N T	S I N G H	R A J P U T	
3+6+3+5+1+5+4	3+1+5+3+5	2+1+1+8+6+4	
27 +	17 +	22	=66

Date of Birth: January 21, 1986

1+21+1986   =46

Sushant was born under a very strong Sun influence that brought fame and success on a large scale. Numbers 3 and 6 were the numbers that worked best for him based on his date of birth. As indicated, his full name adds up to a 66 that contradicts his name vibration. The name gave him an overdose of Venus energy that attracted love affairs and created many hidden enemies. He entered his 35th year in the year 2020 and that fact was also in conflict with the number 66 in his name vibration. I feel that the reason for his sudden passing ultimately goes back to his name vibration.

His first name and middle name add up to a 44 which accelerated the heavy energy after he entered his 35th birthday. Unfortunately, his last name was not in his favor and tipped the scales against him in the year 2020. The example of Sushant highlights the importance of name energies and how they can be catalysts for success or bring unnecessary and unexplained challenges that end in tragedy. His name energy attracted other numbers like an apartment number 601 and a motorcycle with license plate number 4848. These were both too heavy for his name energy.

I use the Chaldean code to calculate numbers. There are many other codes out there but I find this one to be the most accurate. We can improve our quality of life by knowing which numbers work best for us and then harmonizing our lives with those numbers through our home and business addresses, business names, bank account numbers, telephone numbers, license plates, and so on.

I would also like to highlight the importance of sun signs and the numbers that rule them:

Aries	9
Taurus	6
Gemini	5
Cancer	2
Leo	1
Virgo	5
Libra	6
Scorpio	9
Sagittarius	3
Capricorn	8
Aquarius	4 and 8
Pisces	3

The date of birth and its family of numbers should also be taken into consideration for calculating name energy. For example, a number 8 birthday should not have a name vibration that adds up to a 4 or 8. Instead the numbers 1, 3, and 5 are considered auspicious. Fire and air elements work well with one another while earth and water elements connect. For example, the earth sign Capricorn works better with a water sign like Scorpio than a fire sign like Aries, though both of these carry the energy of number 9.

As evidenced by the high divorce rates in our world, plenty of couples find themselves in challenging relationships. If the basic numbers between the partners don't match, it then becomes advisable to balance the name vibrations so that their names are compatible. I have seen famous celebrities in tough relationships, but their name vibrations kept them together to remain in the same home and raise their children successfully.

Numbers 3, 6, and 9 are compatible with one other. On the other end, numbers 1, 2, 4, and 7 work well together. Number 5 is a neutral number that works well with the number 8 but not so well with the number 9. Please consider this information when creating new names or correcting existing name energies. Based on my many years of reading numbers, my belief is that the Chaldean code I use in my personal practice works better than other methods.

Numbers and Timing

Knowing the right time to execute plans is critical for their success. We can attain this knowledge simply by looking at our numbers; they can tell us when the time is most ripe to achieve our goals. Depending on our dates of birth, there are certain months out of every year that bring luck and some that simply won't work no matter how much effort we put in.

Numerological timing is very important because it helps us understand the peak of good and bad timing. Sometimes our business is doing well and then suddenly things start changing rapidly because of new competition or market conditions. The timing of making money and getting out at the right time is crucial. Many people who mastered these principles never had to work again.

In the early 1990s I met a gentleman from Silicon Valley who became immensely successful in the tech business in a short period of time. God gave him a huge break. His friend list included big names like then-President Bill Clinton and First Lady Hillary Clinton.

He lived in a mansion that carried a huge price tag. One day, a prospective buyer who was interested in buying his property knocked his door. Being the end of the year and holiday season, the initial offer was revised with a higher offer. This made the seller seriously contemplate the offer. Tempted by the higher amount, the seller sold his home. Unfortunately, he also sold was his luck. He bought another property soon after, but things were never the same again. He never prospered again. His holdings plummeted with many badly-timed business decisions. Desperately trying to make a comeback, he passed away while on an unnecessary business trip to a faraway country. This man didn't understand timing and because of it, his life ended prematurely. Had he continued to stay in his former home, he would have been a happy person right now.

Lucky Months for Your Number

If the number 1 appears in your date of birth, the months of February, July, August, and December are the best months for you. Your luck will be highest during these months and good things will manifest quite easily for you. Sell a house or start a new project or relationship during these months, as the energies will support your endeavors.

If the number 2 is your number, it means that the Moon rules you and enhances your intuition. Mid-year is most favorable: May, June, July, and August are the months when you'll find yourself happier and more successful.

If the number 3 happens to be your number, then you can bring your wishes to life most easily during March, May, October, November, and December. I say this from personal experience as I'm a number 3 and I always look forward to these months.

If the number 4 is your number, then May, July, August, and October are your best months. You should be cautious in the first two months of the year. Sit still and reflect until your months roll around.

If the number 5 is your number, then May, June, September, and December are your most fortunate months. Bollywood star Amir Khan carries this energy and always launches his new projects in the month of December that have been huge hits.

If the number 6 happens to be your number, then March, May, October, November, and December are your most advantageous months. This number carries the energy of planet Venus and is luckier than other numbers.

If the number 7 happens to be your number, then February, June, July, and August are your lucky months. Mr. Arvind Kejriwal, the Chief Minister of New Delhi, has this number in his code. He's won the election four times in a row because they take place in the month of February each time. The ruling party has tried hard to unseat him, but their attempts have been futile. These are the kinds of victories that your best time can bring for you.

If the number 8 happens to be your number, then the months of March, May, June, August, and December will make your luck shine. This number carries the energy of slow-moving planet Saturn and works well with Mercury and Venus energies.

If the number 9 happens to be your number, then March, April, May, November, and December are your most auspicious months.

Months that resonate with your date of birth are peak times for bigger and better things to happen for you. Maybe you're trying to handle a complex situation or settle a legal matter, buy a home or a vehicle, or start a new business or job. Learn when the time is best, and act in that time.

I get many calls from people who gamble and have questions about enhancing their success rate. Personally, I don't gamble and do not have any advice for gamblers, as my life was full of challenges that I had to overcome with no shortcuts, only conviction and hard work.

I had a client one time who was in the construction business and she was having a lucky streak gambling in casinos from Reno to Vegas. She sounded thrilled each time she came to see me about buying more properties. She was pushing her luck until one day she incurred this huge bill that forced her to sell her own property, which had been built by The husband after years of toil. She also set a poor example for her children, who wanted to do as their mother had done and get rich quickly in the wrong business. Her oldest son even had to spend time behind bars. Timing is important for doing positive things, but there's no good time to do wrong.

I have an East Indian couple that I've been working with for a number of years now. The wife is a yoga teacher and a consultant, and the husband used to work in a large Silicon Valley corporation for many years. Both of their children are well-educated and happily settled down. I met them for a consultation in the last quarter of 2019. The husband had been laid off from his job and wasn't sure if he would find new employment soon. They were debating selling their home. "Is it the right thing to do?" they asked me. Per their numbers, it happened to be the right time to sell and I suggested that they get rid of the house and downsize or rent for the time being. They agreed and listed the property, which sold well over the asking price. This proved that their time was conducive for the sale of a property. After a few months of renting, the realtor who was representing them found them another house that would fit their budget. My clients loved the property and called me to ask my opinion on the address of the house and the city in which it was located. I told them that the house did not work well with them. They were not too happy but agreed not to put in an offer. They even had the realtor call me to convince me but that didn't work. One week later, my clients called me again to tell me that they had found out the selling agent misrepresented some of the disclosures. They were happy they didn't get stuck in what would've been a bad deal. They continued looking and I reassured them that the perfect home would appear as soon as their time was right.

The right time came during the first week of July 2020. Despite the pandemic that was sweeping the world, a great property appeared. My clients got the house in a multiple offer situation. They were thrilled to finally have their dream retirement home.

I have a friend who's a lawyer who came to the US around the same time I did. Over the years, I've recommended people to him to avail of his services. Like most lawyers, he's intelligent and analytical and we often end up talking about a lot of different subjects as we've both been to different countries in our lifetimes. His love for flying is undying and he's keen on discussing this topic with me as I've been a commercial pilot and flight instructor.

The only problem is that he's not very *good* at it. My friend has flown with many instructors in different flight schools in the San Francisco Bay Area but has been unable to complete sufficient flight time to be signed off by his instructor for a check ride. His flight instructors gauge him quickly because he's highly educated and new ones keep coming.

I've told him on numerous occasions to stop flying and concentrate on his legal profession, as I strongly feel that he's risking his and his instructor's lives because flying is just not his forte. His time to learn how to fly has long come and gone but my persistent friend doesn't want to take my advice. Time will tell (as it always does).

You must know in what days, months, and years to do and refrain from doing certain things. Being a number 3, I avoid doing anything important in the months of January and February. This pattern repeats every year and I'm already aware of it. I have learned some important life lessons in the past during these months that have made me very conscious. Every year between Christmas and New Year's Day, I try not to drive as some strange things happen on the road that I can't explain. Then as the winter season fades and spring comes, things begin to shift. Every year in the month of March, I end up overcoming a challenge and coming out as a winner. The month of May always pulls more money and the last three months of the year are always highly productive for me. Spring and fall always work well for me. I have indicated the best months for different dates of birth in earlier paragraphs. Observe them carefully and you'll be surprised at the things you will learn about yourself.

The timing of important decisions is crucial for success and to prevail in difficult situations. Know your time, work with your time, and use your time wisely.

Home Numbers Bring Luck

Certain metaphysical principles have been used extensively for buying or selling homes or for adjusting the energies of spaces to attract success and prosperity and live in harmony with the flow of nature. The first one is Feng Shui, a system widely practiced in the Far East. I remember in the early 1990's when the concept of Feng Shui swept the Western World. It has many schools, but the one that become very popular is the Bagua system. Bagua means an octagon placed over any place of business or residence where each point of the Bagua has an element connected to it. Energies of money, partnership, creativity, knowledge, and children can be adjusted by applying the Bagua system. If the space is having money issues, the far-left corner of the space is adjusted or if a business is struggling with employees, the right side of the entry point is improved by adding light to lift that energy. The center point of the space is highly important and often light fixtures or crystals are hung to keep the place centered.

Another principle is Vaastu Shastra that comes from the Vedic tradition and has been implemented for thousands of years. It has gained a lot of popularity after big business names have used it to promote their businesses. Vaastu is based on the thought that the five elements of water, fire, air, earth, and space must be balanced. Just as the human body breathes in and out comfortably, when all elements in a space are balanced the home breathes effortlessly and the flow of energies entering the space brings only good things to the home. If something is off, the placing of the five elements needs to be adjusted. In this popular system, the northeast direction is considered auspicious for spirituality and gaining wealth.

The third system I have been practicing for many years is the science of numerology. As a licensed real estate broker in the state of California, I have had the opportunity to buy and sell many properties for my clients over the years. When the energies of buyers are matched with the properties, my clients can make huge equities. The technique of number patching also explained in this book has proven to be very beneficial for my clients.

One example comes to mind. Many years ago, I was visiting an open house for a property in a very elite area of Fremont, California. This property was listed for over two million dollars. As usual, the first thing I noted as I entered the property was the number, which I did not like. The real estate agent mentioned that the property was well-tuned using the principles of Feng Shui. A Koi pond inside the property had some very expensive Koi fish imported from Japan. The owners of this property were business people but despite all their effort, they had to leave the home and it went back to the lender. Before one buys a property, it is imperative that all aspects of the property be considered. One's own due diligence and intuition are truly important before an informed decision is made in buying a property.

Numbers and their different shades have to be considered carefully. When I look at numbers, I view them as planetary energy. Say, for example, that you come and consult with me and you are told that one of the numbers that complement you is a number 6. As many know, number 6 is planet Venus that represents the color blue and is great for love and money and the more positive elements of life. With this newfound knowledge, you go looking for a home and the real estate agent finds you a property with 8484 as its number. After you add the numbers, it reduces to a number 6 and you're happy because you know that 6 is one of your numbers. Would this be the right buy? Buying a property based on this is definitely not a good idea because in these numbers, the planetary energy of Saturn (number 8) and

Uranus (number 4) is repeated twice and this causes a downward spiral and affects all the members of the family.

The search starts again and the real estate agent finds another property with the number 501. Content, you rush to make the deal. This again would not be a good buy as Mercury (number 5) preceding the Sun (number 1) does not work well. You might have heard of Area 51 in the mountains of Nevada where the US Government conducts all kind of military testing as shown in many television documentaries.

Another property you might look at has the number 9951. This will once more reduce to a number 6 but again carries very heavy energies. Number 9, carrying the energy of planet Mars, repeats twice followed by number 5, carrying the energy of Mercury, and 1, carrying the energy of the Sun. These planets don't work well together and this is not a good idea. I can give you many such examples with other numbers, but I believe you get the point. Consider number combinations carefully before arriving at any conclusions.

Some good shades of number 6 energy are the numbers 24, 42, and 33. I have personally experienced the energies of these numbers and they have always worked well for me. Please remember that these are just examples. Ultimately, one's number chart needs to be analyzed in order to find his or her most favorable numbers.

Often I have clients who are so fixated in finding the exact number that their desperation blocks the energy of attracting the best vibration for them. My advice to you is to relax and allow the Universe to direct the best energy towards you. This can only happen if one is calm, collected, and focused and knows that the universe will help (the universe always wants to help us!). Rushing to buy is never a good idea. I had a client who consulted with me many times and was in a hurry to buy a second home in the San Francisco Bay Area. The home that he was living in was not the best either, but I recommended a number patch and this did improve things. I understood his haste: he was awaiting his father's arrival from India and rushed into buying another home.

I received a call from him one day to have a consultation. He asked me about the number that he had bought and I was unhappy to hear the address. "You should have asked me before buying," I told him. He told me what happened. Soon after his father arrived from India to be with him and his family, the father had a major heart attack and had to be hospitalized. He made some mistakes in his investments and was drained financially. His daughter also had some health issues and was not doing that well. "It all happened so quickly," he said.

Please don't hurry to make changes to your residence, as the move can present many challenges if not done correctly. If the numbers don't work for you, they can actually create more problems.

I've also had clients in the past who moved from smaller to bigger homes only to find out that they left their luck in the smaller home. If a home is working for you, it's a good idea not to change it.

Travelling and Numbers

We all travel for various purposes including business and pleasure. Travelling takes us to different countries and cities and in different hotels and resorts. I believe that a room number should be in tune with one's energy. I have personally experienced this many times. I always choose hotels and request for room numbers that make me feel comfortable and that I know work for me. We've all experienced happy trips and not so happy ones, and one of the reasons for this is the places we choose to stay. A longtime client of mine ended up in the ER instead of Disneyland during one of her trips with her grandkids. She recounted her experience to me and I recognized that the timing she had chosen to travel was not the best one. Please stay within the boundaries of your best numbers during your outings to create fun and memorable trips.

Whether one is travelling for business, pleasure, or simply going on vacation, the success of the trip will have a lot to do with its numerological timing: Do the dates and destination flow with the traveler's AstroNumerology chart? It is well known that planning to take a trip or going on a journey while Mercury is retrograde is never a good idea. Any trips undertaken during this period are bound to cause delays, confusion, and a lot of miscommunication. The energy of the destination (e.g., "Hawaii") and where the traveler will stay (a specific hotel, resort, bed and breakfast, etc.) can also determine the traveler's happiness and satisfaction with the journey. Therefore, it is essential to check the AstroNumerological "weather" forecast before making any travel plans. Besides initiating trips during the right period, days and dates that conform to one's own AstroNumerological numbers should be carefully considered.

I have learned this from experience. In one of my trips to India to meet my family, a relative requested that I bring him a Golf Set. I picked one up from a local store but on arrival in New Delhi the customs decided to impose a duty that was way over the price of the item. I showed them the receipt that I carried with me but they refused to believe me saying that such receipts can be easily made. They gave me an option to leave the item at the storage and take it back to the States on my way out. That is exactly what happened. The item came back with me and the store clerk who sold the item to me complained but gave me a refund. I later realized that I had made the purchase during a mercury retrograde period. Please make your travel plans carefully for enjoyable trips.

I have met people from all walks of life and keep meeting new ones regularly from around the world. Zoom calls are the in thing and connecting via video calls for business has made the world even smaller. It makes me very happy to hear from clients at a distance who have used my information to better their lives. Many find my first book interesting and some miss the point, which is fine. Some clients seem to have a lot of knowledge but never reached the point of success they desire. They consult with me but still keep chasing their tails. Many just like to copy other people to be like them and continue in the struggling mode. Then there have been some in the past that just drained my energy. I remember an intuitive that was introduced to me through a common friend in Los Angeles. She consulted with famous people and kept calling me for help in finding the right address in the West LA area. Each time after I spoke with her, I had massive headaches. I later wondered what kind of person she was and completely cut her out. I have had other clients that I consulted in the film and television business and found them to be very insecure. I have learned so much from all the people the Universe sends to me and I continue to provide to them my very best.

Adding numbers is not always a good idea. There are several different kinds of numerology; each has its particular strengths. However, even the best system is worthless without clear and consistent interpretation relative to the issues at hand.

With clarity, insight, and compassion, I have consulted with individuals regarding their personal and business lives.

I use the term AstroNumerology because I associate numbers with planets, which are astronomical bodies. AstroNumerology is not about adding numbers up; it is about looking at each individual number, since each represents a particular planet, and considering the totality of the number's own "planetary system." Each planet is further associated with different precious & semiprecious gems, and colors, and the planets share relationships with each other within the Solar System.

Adding a certain number to improve the vibration of a home or business (known as "patching") is like adding the energy of another planet to that particular place. Most homes or businesses are patched very specifically, based on the type of business or the date(s) of birth and names(s) of the person(s) living in the residence.

Adding numbers adds complexity. As I have indicated, each number has a planetary energy associated with it. I have seen that many times, people still make mistakes when it comes to picking addresses, despite knowing their best numbers. One such client of mine who worked in Silicon Valley could not understand why his son was lagging in his education. Soon after I suggested a patch, the energy shifted and things improved. My client was looking to buy a house and suddenly felt that he knew it all. Knowing the best numbers for the family, the husband and wife picked a home in a new subdivision in the San Francisco Bay area and rented the one that was patched. It is always a good idea to move to a newer energy. I got a call from my client a month after he had moved into the property and in which he stated that he wanted to meet with me urgently. I was not aware of his move until I met him again. During our consultation, he told me how he and his wife had decided to buy this new home. My client also mentioned that he felt insecure in his job after he had made the change. So although he picked the right number by adding all the digits of the home number, the individual numbers of the house did not carry an energy that was favorable to the family. I was not surprised and suggested a fix.

Let's look into how each individual number in an address affects the energy of the property and those living in it. If number 3 happens to be your best vibration, this number will not be the best one and I'll explain why.

Let's say the home address is 37884. These numbers add up to a number 30. An amateur will say that this is a good number because it adds to a 3 vibration with 0 being an amplifier. That is not true. Besides the number 3 in the combination, the numbers 7884 are all contradictory planets represented by Neptune, Saturn twice, and Uranus. These planetary vibrations do not work with the number 3 and living in a home with this address will attract many financial and relationship blocks and even health challenges. There are many other good combinations that will work well with a number 3 vibration. I have a celebrity friend who lives in a house number 111 in Mumbai, India. The home is in complete sync with her date of birth. Her fame and success have risen significantly since she moved into this house.

Now let's say that 5 happens to be your best number and you consider this energy as a home or office. Let's take the address 35474. This combination adds to a number 23, a vibration that flows with a number 5. But only the number 5 in the combination works. The other numbers, 3474, contradict the energy of number 5 and moving to such a home number is, again, not a good idea. If by chance the number happens to be a 5450, the energy is more beneficial. I picked this number randomly, but there are many other combinations that would also work well.

My first book has been widely read. Many call me after reading it for a consultation and many tried to teach my method to others after reading it. I appreciate their gestures so long as the information was interpreted correctly to help and not confuse people.

Bank Account Numbers Bring Luck

Banks and bank account numbers play a very important role in our lives. We all need money to pay our bills and save for the future. Over the years consulting clients and coming to understand the energy of money, I have realized that banks must flow with our own energies and our bank account numbers should also vibrate with our frequency to attract and keep money in them.

I'm sure we can all recall that in the past we had certain bank accounts that always had money in them. And then there were accounts in which money never stayed for too long. From experience I can tell you that the name and address of our banking institutions also must correlate with our own personal energies to attract money into our accounts.

Having lived in the West and consulted with many clients over the years, I have seen people from the Far East sit with bank executives and look at different account numbers based on their belief system before opening accounts. I personally believe that if the energy of the bank is flowing with you, the right account number will be attracted to you

I also believe that opening accounts during a rising moon period on a Friday (being the day of planet Venus in one's own lucky cycle) is a good idea. I have discussed lucky months for different numbers in this book.

The number eight seems to be very popular with people from the Far East. They prefer this number to repeat in their bank account numbers. It is important to understand that the number eight is a number that does not work with everybody. Please do not follow people blindly when looking at account numbers as your energy is different than theirs. It is always good to work with your own numbers when choosing account numbers.

I have had clients who moved from the Far East into prime locations in Los Angeles by finding a property online that was adjoining a bank. One such client of mine moved from Malaysia to Santa Monica, California after finding a property adjoining a bank. I was invited to her house for a personal reading. Her money luck was good but she had serious problems with her relationship and in a couple of years, she would have to exit her marriage. In her case, her house number carried a lot of moon energy that was not matching with her date of birth and living next to a bank did not bring her peace of mind and a stable family life.

During one of my trips to the City of Mumbai, I drove past the home of an A-list actor known globally to see a corner of his home rented to a bank. It didn't surprise me. His fans the world over know his story and I'll leave it at that.

Bank account numbers should be in sync with one's own personal numerology. Sometimes one gets lucky and is assigned a beneficial account number, but many times this is not the case. It's always a good idea to change the account number if it's not pulling in the energy of money.

Bank names and location addresses are also important. They should also work with the energy of one's numerology. Based on my experience, I recommend that the bank name and account numbers should be considered carefully for financial gain and success. Strong business names also complement bank account numbers to attract money into the accounts.

ATM pin numbers that are used for ATM and debit transactions are equally important as they vibrate with one's subconscious mind. The best money numbers can be determined based on one's date of birth.

After reading the above, one might wonder how to check and correct their accounts if they're not working for them. The first step is to become familiar with the number patterns that works for you based on your date of birth. After that, I believe that hard work, good karma, and one's own intuition will hold the answer.

There have been some financial institutions in certain third world countries that have duped all their customers by giving huge unsecured loans to businesses. Those delinquent loans caused immense pain and suffering to the small-time account holders who were ripped of their life savings by unscrupulous bankers. Times are changing in the world and one needs to be very cautious with their hard-earned money.

If you are confused about whether your bank account numbers are positive, one method to get clarity is to add up all the numbers in the account. If the sum of the bank account number adds up to a number 3, 5, or 6, then it has a positive money energy. The number 4 is one number I don't like in a bank account as it's unpredictable and has the tendency to swing downward. If you have a number 1 date of birth, then a bank account number that adds up to a number 1 will also be useful.

As I've mentioned in earlier chapters, I use the Chaldean code to derive the name-number vibrations. Below are some important financial institutions in my part of the world. Let's look at these institutions and their name-numbers:

C I T I		B A N K	
3+1+4+1		2+1+5+2	
9	+	10	=19

W E L L S		F A R G O	
6+5+3+3+3		8+1+2+3+7	
20	+	21	=41

B A N K		O F		A M E R I C A	
2+1+5+2		7+8		1+4+5+2+1+3+1	
10	+	15	+	17	=42

	U N I O N		B A N K	
	6+5+1+7+5		2+1+5+2	
	24	+	10	=34

	U S		B A N K	
	6+3	+	2+1+5+2	
	9	+	10	=19

	C H A S E	
	3+5+1+3+5	=17

The energy of Chase flows well with the vibration of 2021. It will become stronger after the middle of 2021 and also work well in 2022.

If number 1 happens to be your best number then the number 19 should work for you. Let's look at the examples above. Both Citibank and US Bank carry the same vibration. They both add up to a 19. If I were to choose between these two names, US Bank would be my choice. The reason is because of the combination of numbers 6 and 3 in "US". Venus and Jupiter are always better at drawing in the energy of money than the number 9 that Citibank adds up to.

If you have a 3 date of birth you should stay away from the vibration that carries the energy of number 34. This vibe will not attract a good bank account for you. On the other hand, if you have a number 1 or 2 vibration, then this number will work well for you.

If you have a number 5 or 8 vibration, then you should stick to the 41 or 42 bank name vibration as shown above. These institutions will attract more money luck for you.

If you have a number 6 vibration in your energy, then the bank numbers adding up to 41 or 42 will work well for you. Try to find banks that are accessible and have lots of parking spaces. I have seen many banks in tight corners that constantly attract angry customers complaining about lousy customer service. This is not a good energy for money overall. Also check colors of bank logos and compare them to your own number vibrations. I have written about numbers and colors in this book.

Social Security numbers are a part of our identities as US citizens and everyone who lives legally in the United States is assigned one. By adding up the nine digits on your Social Security card, you'll find that the total number might or might not be favorable for you. These numbers are automatically generated by the Social Security department and getting a good one is a luck of the draw. Unfortunately, this number cannot be changed and is used in all official applications including applying for loans, mortgages, credit cards, and opening new bank accounts. I believe that each individual's Social Security number plays an important role in influencing the energy of money into or out of his or her bank account.

Telephone Numbers Bring Luck

Telephone numbers are an inseparable part of our day-to-day existence. We all have a phone number, whether it's a cellphone or landline, and we use phone numbers to stay in touch with our loved ones. The phone numbers assigned to us carry certain vibrations and work favorably when they resonate with our planetary energies. The application of numbers in everyday life can be truly complicated, but life-changing.

A popular combination of numbers that's desired by many people from the Far East includes the number 8. Many people prefer to have their phone number end with the number 8. Eight is the energy of planet Saturn and represents the symbol of infinity. It is widely believed that having the number 8 in a phone number is a good number for business and business people. Personally, I believe that a heavy dose of this number slows down the energy as it's represented by Saturn, a cold planet.

Because telephones are a means of communication, the presence of number 5 is good to keep the energy flowing. Many media outlets have the energy of number 5 in their numbers. Number 5 is represented by the energy of the fast-moving planet Mercury. As this mode of communication involves fast flow of energy, the presence of the Sun, number 1, and Mars, number 9, are also recommended for names of businesses that sell telecommunication devices and equipment.

Telephone numbers tend to confuse people and often I get calls from my clients to find the right numbers for them. Upon request, most phone companies will provide the subscriber a set of numbers to pick from. It's always smart to know your numbers because it's best to stick with numbers that attract good vibrations and flow with your date of birth.

A client who moved from London to Mumbai, India to pursue her dream in the film industry consulted with me for a reading. After looking at some options, I suggested to her a phone number that would bolster her career. I was glad to see her in some big budget films later on.

Another client who consulted with me worked for a large company that relocated from New York to San Jose, California. She had been following me on my YouTube channel for several years and like many others, had picked a phone number with which she wasn't happy and insisted that I help her out. After looking at the choices she was given, I suggested a new combination for her connection. After a couple of weeks, she started getting the calls she had been hoping for after interviewing for some big companies in Silicon Valley. She later decided to become an entrepreneur and start her own company.

There are businesses that sell phones as well as service the damage that happens to them (we're all aware of what happens to an iPhone when water gets inside it). I suggest that the names and addresses for telecom companies should have more Sun and

Mars energy. Personally, I like to use a red cover on my phone as it carries the energy of Mars and also works with my own numbers.

The number 5 carries the energy of fast-moving planet Mercury and also represents communication. I've observed that more use of the numbers 5 and 8 in a phone number keeps the phone ringing with good calls. This combination works quite well for business people. Phones can also be programmed to attract more calls using crystals. This is usually done by keeping the phone near preprogrammed crystals that attract the right energy and keep it ringing. Red colored phones carry the energy of Mars and ring more often because of warm energy. In my experience, black covers or phones hold heavier energies and should be avoided as they're more likely to fall and get damaged.

The numbers 999 in a phone number mean heavy energy. This combination works well for hospitals, police departments, and other types of medical facilities and law enforcement agencies. However, I don't recommend having this combination for regular use. If this combination happens to be in your phone number, consider getting the number changed (I say this from personal experience). As a young officer in the Indian Army, I had a 99 extension on my phone number. I remember the phone always had issues and constant technical help did not fix the problem, even after the device was changed. Since then, I like to stay away from multiples of 9 in my phone number. Being a fire sign, number 9 by itself has always worked well for me. The combination of 444 should also be avoided in phone numbers as it attracts useless calls that are irritating to the recipient.

Passcodes are often set on our smart devices. It's always a good idea to set a code that flows with your personal numbers. For example, an 8 date of birth should use the 3, 6, or 5 family of numbers and avoid using the numbers 8 or 4. A good example for passcodes would be the combination 5550 or 3650 for people with the number 8 in their code. Other favorable combinations can be determined by looking at different dates of birth. The right numbers work with the subconscious mind and attract good luck and prosperity.

Wallpapers on phones should also be chosen carefully. They should represent success, financial gains, or positive affirmations. We keep our phones with us at all times and although we may not realize it, we see the background and wallpaper of our phone dozens of times each day! Our subconscious mind becomes programmed accordingly. With so many companies that sell communication devices these days, it's always a good idea to match the numerology of the manufacturer to one's own energy to stay in the flow.

Let's look at an example of how to harmonize energy using phone numbers:

$$J \ O \ H \ N \qquad\qquad D \ O \ E$$
$$1+7+5+5 \qquad\qquad 4+7+5$$
$$18 \qquad + \qquad 16 \qquad =34$$

Date of Birth: January 6, 1975
$$1+6+22 \qquad\qquad =29$$

Telephone Number:
$$925+355+8732 \qquad =49$$

If we look at this example, John Doe has a name vibration of number 34. This number does not connect with his date of birth on the 6th or with the sign he is born under. Capricorn is ruled by number 8 which carries the energy of restrictive planet Saturn. The number 6 in his date of birth flows with the number 8 and that's a good sign. His phone number adds up to a number 49, further reduced to a number 4. This phone number doesn't work with the number 6 in his day of birth or the number 7 that rules his name vibration. The numbers 29 and 49 can work together. This phone number is a 50 percent energetic match for John Doe and he would do well to get a different number.

If the phone number changes to 925 355 8733, which equals 50, the entire vibration changes favorably for John Doe. The number 50 works well with the numbers 8 and 6 that appear in his chart. Being a neutral vibration, it can also balance the other numbers. This would be a much better number match for John Doe.

Phone numbers adding up to the 1 or 5 family can be used. Zero is an amplifier as it further enhances the energy of the total phone vibrations. It would be better if it didn't appear at all in the phone number, as it doesn't generate any planetary energy.

One last thought is to keep the content as clean as possible. Messages that carry heavy energy should be deleted as soon as possible so as to remain in a positive state of mind.

Cars and Numbers Bring Luck

Having consulted with innumerable people over the years, I can tell you that the cars we drive have a definite impact on our luck factor. There are three factors I feel should be considered when buying a new car.

The first one is the color of the car. The reason the color of the car we drive is important is because colors are represented by planetary energy and those energies must match the basic energies of the owner. Let me give you an example.

If one has a lot of Saturn energy in one's code, colors like blue, beige, and off-white would match that energy. It's not recommended for people carrying Saturn energy to drive dark-colored cars like black or red, as they contradict their frequencies. If one has a lot of Mars energy, then colors like white or off-white work well. The color of your car must harmonize with the energy encoded in your date of birth for luck and success.

The second factor that must be considered is the make of the car. It doesn't matter if one can afford an expensive car if it doesn't work well with one's energy. The make or brand of the car must also flow with our energy. Tesla might work for some but not for others. A Lexus or BMW might work for some but not for others. The reason behind this is that these names carry different vibrations and whatever one decides to buy must match his or her energy. Business people need to keep their phones ringing even while driving as it's very important for good messages to pour in and this can only happen when one is driving under the right energy. When I think about this, two examples come to mind.

I was in New Delhi one time and a prominent lawyer who had consulted with me many times in the past called me about buying a new car. He told me that his current car would always get hit even when it was parked outside his house. He didn't understand why this kept happening to him. He had a lot of Saturn energy in his chart and a lighter color was better for him. After talking to me, he sold his car and started looking for a new one. The right car took a few months to find, but he was able to get a beige color that was ideal for his date of birth. Some months later, he contacted me to tell me how lucky he felt after getting the new car. His family felt more connected and united, too. This is what the right color car can do for you.

Some years ago, I got a call from a lady who's quite prominent in the Hollywood film industry. She had read my book and wanted a reading. After looking at her date of birth and her personal timing, I concluded that she had a strong Mars influence. However, this energy was not suitable for her and I asked what color was her car. After she told me that she drove a red car, I immediately suggested that it was not a good idea. Soon after, she told me that her boyfriend had gifted her a very expensive red Porsche. She mentioned that right after she had gotten the red Porsche, the car was rear-ended on the 405 freeway in Los Angeles. A red car getting hit during a Mars period on a Mars freeway (the 405) did not surprise me at all. The information I provided made sense to this intelligent lady and she made the changes I suggested.

After immigrating to the United States many years ago, I needed a driver's license to get to and from work. A friend of mine taught how me to drive in his burgundy Toyota pickup truck. After a few lessons, I made my appointment with the local DMV and passed in my first attempt to get my license. It did not dawn on me for a while that the color of the vehicle and the name Toyota both worked with my energy and it made it easy for me to get my license.

After getting my license, I bought a used Chevy Nova from a small dealership in Northern California and it happened to be the color burgundy again. This car just happened to come to me and it helped me move to the San Francisco Bay Area. One evening while driving back from San Jose on a busy freeway, the engine suddenly caught fire. After I pulled over, a California Highway Patrol officer who was a few cars behind me helped me move my personal belongings to his car and later dropped me home. The car was completely gutted. On a later day, after assessing the damage, the insurance company compensated me with more than the value of the car. Again, the color that was my vibration worked for me in a mysterious way.

Many people I know relate the energy of cars to the planet Venus and buy white-colored cars, as this color represents Venus. It's considered auspicious and many celebrities and businessmen are often seen driving white cars for this reason.

The next time you're out looking for a new car because you're not happy with the one you have, I suggest considering your energy and your numbers. Besides due diligence, you can attract success, abundance, and prosperity to you at all times by driving the right energy. Planet Venus represents the energy of love, money, and luxury cars. Most people who drive luxury cars have a strong influence of Venus in their charts.

The third factor to take into consideration is the car's license plate numbers. License plates are equally important to draw in the right energy Sometimes the numbers on our license plates don't match our energies. In a situation like this, I recommend private license plate numbers that can be easily attained by paying a small yearly fee. These plates will help you attain better number vibrations to improve your luck while operating the car.

$$T \quad O \quad Y \quad O \quad T \quad A$$
$$4+7+1+7+4+1 \quad =24$$

$$B \quad M \quad W$$
$$2+4+6 \quad =12$$

M E R C E D E S
4+5+2+3+5+4+5+3   =31

T E S L A
4+5+3+3+1   =16

License Plates

Let's look at a license plate number to calculate its energy.

3 A T K 6 1 6
3+1+4+2+6+1+6   =23

This number would work well with a person who has a 5, 6, or 8 date of birth. Number 2 and 7 people should avoid such a number. The color of a car that's carrying this number should not be red or white. The color, license plate, and make of the car should also be matched to one's energy.

Most people don't know this and some don't care. I can tell you from experience that these numbers are very important to draw in the right energy and increase our luck. Many cars, even if they're in excellent condition, cause trouble for their owners by requiring constant trips to the workshop. Many get pulled over for minor traffic violations time and again and many get into accidents that could've been avoided. From my experience, this happens because the license plate numbers don't work with the owner or driver of the car. I'm often contacted by clients who want to get personalized license plates that are compatible with their vibrations. We see cars with personalized plates all the time.

One should also be careful with personalized license plates; the numbers 8 and 9 should be avoided in any combination. The energy of Mercury, the number 5, works well on cars and should be used in combinations with other numbers considering one's date of birth. Planet Mars, represented by the number 9 and the color red, is not a good idea to have on a plate as I've seen many clients with this number on their plate involved in accidents. Many people from the Far East are very fond of the number 8 that represents Saturn's energy, but it's not a good idea to have this number on a car if one also has that energy in his or her date of birth. I recommend number 8 people avoid black and red cars and stick to lighter-colored cars instead for safety and personal success. The Chinese don't like the number 4 and license plates in China aren't allowed to use that number. Maybe this is because they've become more familiar with that number after the pandemic that devastated the world in 2020 (which adds up to a 4).

An attorney who rented my office for many years had an accident in the San Francisco bay Area many years ago. She knew that I was passionate about numbers and wanted my opinion on a new car and the license plate it should have. I remember utilizing numbers that best fit her energy and she was quite happy with her personalized license plate and the color of her Mercedes-Benz.

NASCAR is a stock car racing company that's popular in the United States and many other advanced countries, since racing is a dream for many people. The colors of cars and the numbers they carry have to vibrate with the driver for success. I had a chance to review one such NASCAR event and the findings were published in a popular sports magazine.

I have a client who is Austrian and chose to convert to Hinduism. He knows a lot about Hindu practices and has spent time in various spiritual centers. In fact, I was surprised at how much knowledge he had about the Hindu religion. He found me online and we spoke over Zoom. Born on August 16, he was very intuitive and listened intently. During the course of the reading, I told him that he should never drive a black car. He was surprised and told me that on two occasions in the past, he owned black cars and both of them were wrecked in accidents. His story serves to show that the color of the car we drive is important not only for our success, but our safety. He says that ever since he switched to a white car, he's felt luckier. It serves every one of us to drive a car whose color and numbers resonate with our highest energies for success.

CHAPTER TWO

HEAVY NUMBERS AND HEALING ENERGIES

Heavy Numbers

From years of experience consulting thousands of people, I learned about certain heavy number energies whose characteristics and influence on our lives should be understood.

The first of these numbers is 16. This number has Sun and Venus energy, which is not a favorable combination. Homes that have this number attract miscommunication and situations like treachery and deception. It also brings health challenges from the waist down and loss from money and fire. I have seen many people who carry this energy in their names, dates of birth, or home addresses lose their lives in fire-related accidents. I strongly recommend that homes and apartments that carry the number 16 be patched with the right energy to raise the vibration for better luck and abundance. Placing the element of water at the right place also helps in balancing the energy of this number. As I write this book, a famous young Indian film actor was found dead under very mysterious circumstance in his flat number 601 in Mumbai, India. His date of birth did not work with the number 601. This number impacts the area below the stomach and down to the feet. Initial investigations and medical reports suggest that the celebrity suffered a broken leg and other injuries on his legs. This did not surprise me, as I have seen such energy repeating with clients that I consulted over the years. I've also seen fire suddenly erupting in the kitchen area in homes with such numbers as well as the lingering energy of deception present within the home.

The second of these numbers is 18. This number carries the energy of the Sun and planet Saturn. Over the years, I have met numerous clients who have experienced the negative energies of this number. It benefits people who are in the medical field or in law enforcement. Residents of homes that carry this number often face health challenges and relationship issues. I strongly recommend that this number be patched with the right energies to minimize the negative effects of planet Mars. The city of Mumbai in India is also the financial capital of India. The name of the city used to be Bombay, but soon after the name changed the energy changed with it. The new name, Mumbai, carries heavy Mars energy that has turned the city into a center of crime and lawlessness ruled by hidden interests. The assault on the famous Taj Hotel by terrorists happened only after the name change. The media is constantly bombarded with mysterious deaths of famous people and stories of the nexus of the mafia. Members of law enforcement and corrupt politicians are constantly in the news. Names of people or cities need to be changed carefully so as to maintain a positive energy.

I have a client in Silicon Valley whom I've known for many years. He is a highly educated man who raised equally educated children who work in high positions. For many years, he lived in a house that carries the energies of the Sun and Saturn, the numbers 1 and 8, respectively. His first wife fell ill and passed away inside the house and later, his daughter's marriage that was solemnized in the same home ended in divorce. Well-versed in Vedic traditions, the man consulted with me but was not satisfied with my answers about patching his home. I consulted with him many times until he was suddenly hit by a stroke. It is inevitable that such number combinations will bring calamities to the inhabitants of the home. The sooner they patch or change the address, the sooner their lives can become more peaceful.

Another such example is of a client whom I met many years ago after coming to America and who still lives in an 18 numbered residence. She was the daughter of a diplomat and was well-educated and has travelled extensively. When we first met, she was divorced and lived in a single-family home in the San Francisco Bay Area. After consulting with me, she didn't care about what I suggested to her. She got remarried to another gentleman who was not as educated as her but a seemingly stable person. After he moved into her home, the couple started having domestic issues and law enforcement had to visit the house more than once. This marriage also ended in a divorce but the woman still refused to leave her home. Many health challenges then followed. Her husband also became my client and he stated that he felt safe and relaxed after leaving that house. He is now happily remarried and stays connected with his children, while the woman continues meeting the same challenges. This goes to show us that the energy of 1 and 8 is a challenging one and that we should be cautious with this number combination.

Number 11 is another challenging number to have on your home or residence. A client of mine who is a successful eye doctor in Southern California contacted me after reading my book. During the reading, I told him that the number 11 was not his number and that it would bring him relationship challenges. He was married but seeing another woman at the same time, which did not surprise me. After suggesting to patch the home with a number that favored all the occupants of the house, his family energy started improving. His business began doing better and the relationship with his spouse recovered. I consult him on a regular

basis and even though he's a medical professional, he now understands the metaphysical aspect of our human existence.

In the summer of 2020, the Indian film industry, commonly
known as Bollywood, erupted in a state of turmoil after the mysterious death of a young male celebrity. I mentioned his home and
motor cycle numbers in this chapter. The main suspect is an actress
who lives in a flat with the number 101 and after researching her
information, I wasn't surprised that her life had become so challenging. The numbers of her residence invited very heavy energies
into her and her family members' lives, including being investigated by various authorities. This combination invites relationship challenges and money issues. Disadvantageous home number
combinations can turn the lives of its occupants upside down.

I have met many intuitives over the years who have consulted me about their home numbers. I've noticed that the majority of them choose the number 11 because they consider it a
master number. In reality, the number 11 on a home address only
makes their lives rife with challenges. This number works better
on a name vibration if it happens to match the energy of one's
date of birth.

Another combination that I find troublesome is the number
135 in any order. I have seen this combination of numbers on
many properties and in all cases, the occupants have struggled
and left these homes. If this happens to be your house number,
please patch the home or find another residence. I say this based
purely on my experience with numbers.

The combination of numbers 4848 is another heavy combination that should be avoided at all times, whether on a residence,
business address, or vehicle license plate. I knew of a person who
was in the metaphysical field and chose this number on a residence
hoping to attract the energy of luck and money, as it adds up to
a 24. But the numbers in this combination actually represent the
energy of the Sun and Saturn colliding and spiraling downwards.
Sadly, this person lost his life in a devastating car accident.

The next time I saw the number 4848 was on the license
plate of a motorcycle that had belonged to the young Bollywood

celebrity I mentioned earlier who passed away in the summer of 2020. Irrespective of where they appear, this is how seriously numbers can impact our lives: sometimes the numbers we choose can make the difference between life and death.

Stay within your own number vibrations for your wellbeing and prosperity. My recommendation is based purely on my extensive research of different number sequences.

The number 14 is a powerful number and moves fast to bring financial success. If it appears with a 0 as an amplifier—e.g. 104 or 140—it becomes even stronger. I have used this energy myself and so have many of my clients. If the home or apartment number happens to carry this energy, it's important to remember that this vibration works for a period of five years and then comes down like a wheel of fortune. Whatever was gained is quickly lost. A wealthy Asian client of mine understands this principle well and has used this number successfully to add more pennies to his portfolio. When the number 14 is overused, it creates a heavy vibration that's no longer beneficial.

The combination of numbers 489 is another difficult energetic combo. Uranus, Saturn, and Mars together make an utterly explosive combination. This number combination should be avoided on homes addresses, business addresses, cars, and other machines.

Healing with Numbers

We all know how important it is for our children to excel in their education so that they can create a bright and secure future for themselves. The first tip I'd like to give to parents is to find the right school or college that resonates with the energy and date of birth of the child. Some children feel uncomfortable in a particular school while others feel happy in it because it aligns with their vibration.

I have a client of Middle Eastern origin who is a successful doctor and married to a heart surgeon living on the East Coast. She's consulted with me many times in the past for various reasons. After the birth of her son, a Capricorn born on January 8, 2000, her anxiety increased. She was overly concerned about the development of her child and about giving her only child the best life and education. She didn't realize that her child had his own life path, his own destiny to fulfill. From the beginning of his education, the child attended the best elementary and preparator schools. The mother insisted that he be admitted to a private school for the elite. Despite his mother's best efforts, the child didn't make it to the preparatory schools of her choice. I received a call from my client one evening requesting a reading. She was sad and distraught. She stated that her son, now a teenager, hated her and liked to spend more time with his father. I was not surprised to hear that, since she had given her son little to no freedom of choice. All of us grow and learn at a different pace.

The number 8 is a slow-moving planet represented by the planet Saturn. The number 8 accounts for a difficult start in life that improves with time. It is therefore very important for people who carry this energy to balance their name vibration with the right numbers. Typically, numbers 1, 5, and 6 work well with the number 8. The colors blue, beige, green, and off-white bring better luck to these people. I have had other clients in the past who have consulted with me but still end up doing what they want, constantly running in circles. Like the lady in my previous example, I've had plenty of over-qualified clients who were unable to raise successful children because they imposed their own expectations and energies upon their children.

The address and city in which the school is located also makes a difference. A few years ago, a client who taught in the Alameda County school district came to consult with me. During the course of the reading, I happened to ask her about the school where she taught. She gave me its address, heavy with Mars energy, and I told her that the cops were visiting her school all the time and she agreed. She was curious to know how I knew that. "It's the address on the door," I said, and she was quite surprised to hear my response. Certain buildings are weighed down with heavy energies and if this happens to be a school, these energies will undoubtedly affect the young minds trying to learn within its walls.

Another important point is the color of clothing. Children attending public schools in the US are mostly free to wear whatever colors they choose while those attending private schools are required to wear a uniform.

I received a call from a lady one night, a physician recovering from the passing of both her husband and son within months of each other. She was a calm and collected, despite the losses she had endured. She told me that she had ordered my book many years ago but had misplaced it. Soon after the passing of her son, the book found her and she instantly felt the need to speak with me. After analyzing her numbers, I realized that she was spiritually elevated and meditated twice a day. She wanted to sell her current house as she felt very lonely but she wanted to confirm the decision with me. I agreed that she should, and soon after I patched the number for her, her home found the right buyers and closed escrow.

My client was also very concerned about her daughter who lived on the East Coast and was married to a businessman who was constantly struggling and had to be supported financially. The son-in-law had built a huge home with a number 8 address. His date of birth was not in sync with the home and he faced many health challenges at that address. My client wanted to help her son-in-law but he refused to believe any advice that she was giving him. During a Thanksgiving visit to his house, my client was able to shift the energy based on my reading, including the energy of the home number. Soon after that, she told me that her son-in-law was considering selling his home and moving. It made her happy and she felt that the change would improve his business and he would be in a position to become self-reliant. Even the most educated people can become blocked. Often they think that being educated is the answer to everything, but that's not the case.

Also important is the room in which a study desk is set up. Some years ago, I spoke with a young lady who had finished medical school in Russia and was struggling to pass the USMLE. After

I consulted with her, she changed the room in which she studied and the direction in which the desk was facing and she was able to pass the required tests. Placing a green lamp on the desk and an amethyst crystal with a clear quartz helps in assimilating information.

One of the many clients I've worked with over the years was a young Muslim lady and mother of two daughters whom I met in the early 1990s. An educationist in her native country, she had been separated from her husband and was working hard to settle in Northern California. She consulted with me often and I felt that she was very intuitive and spiritually advanced. After settling in, she asked me to work with her so that she could buy a townhouse with a low-down payment. The deal worked and she bought her new townhouse. The real estate market then took an upward swing and her equity rose considerably. She sold the property and the profit from it helped her older daughter graduate from UC Berkeley. Whenever she gets stuck, she always calls me and tells me that she feels directed to talk to me and that her problems always get resolved through me. I feel so blessed to know that she sees me as a beacon of luck.

In the spring of 2019, I received a new call from this lady. Her daughter got a new job in a startup company in San Francisco and she insisted that I look for a condo for her daughter facing the Bay. Her daughter had a price in mind and she would not budge. I told the mother that the purchase would not be easy, but she insisted that her prayers had directed her to me again. After looking at some properties, a potential condo appeared close to the Bay. The daughter liked it and submitted an offer. The selling agent happily accepted without a counter offer and the escrow closed well within time. I was surprised at how easily this transaction happened. I am grateful to God that I can be of service to this spiritual family who has complete faith in me and believes their wishes will be granted. In the fall of 2020, I found out that the property my client's daughter had purchased gained over $100,000 in equity. I attributed this to the fact that the condo she bought had the fast-moving energy of number 14.

Once in a while, I get contacted by people who tell me that they've never consulted with anyone but felt driven to talk to me about their numbers. One such person was a businesswoman of many years of East Indian origin who was now living in the UK. Besides owning some retail businesses, I could tell that she was a real estate investor. After dissecting her home address, I told her that the number 2 on her home had been dragging her down. An intelligent woman with excellent personal numbers, she agreed to patch her home with a number 4 to harmonize the energies. Another one of her investments was an apartment complex she had acquired from an auction that had the number 44 and was giving her sleepless nights. This was also patched by my suggestion to make it easy for inspection by the city before the units successfully went out for rent.

I've come across many other investors over the years who, just like this lady, have tried to make a quick buck by buying properties from auctions but end up losing more. The properties acquired either had unknown liens or defects that were only discovered later. My experience with such investments has been bad numbers that caused challenges for the original owners and forced them out of their homes for reasons they didn't understand. Such is the power of numbers, bringing happiness or hardships. The modern buyer is astute, yes, but considering all aspects of a property—including residential and business addresses—is critical for success.

Wearing copper magnetized bracelets are also very effective in enhancing the Sun energy. As the human body grows old, its functions slow down. Wearing this metal helps give more energy to the body.

There is one young lady in the metaphysical business in Southern California who's a great healer and well connected to the rich and famous. Many years ago, when she was still not so known, she got in touch with me to talk about her situation. After reading her numbers and suggesting the right home vibrations, the Universe showed her a place that had the best numbers for her. Since moving, her influence and success have gone up tremendously.

I see young children wear a lot of red and black colors. These are attractive colors, but they don't attract the right energies for education. The color black carries heavy energies of planet Saturn and the color red is tied to Mars energy. Blue is a much better color to gain education as it's a mental color and works with the higher chakras. The colors beige, green, and off-white can also be worn to school to increase mental ability. Gemstones or crystals also help in efficient learning. Depending on the individual's date of birth, the use of ruby, emerald, and yellow sapphire can be considered.

Number Patching

I invented number patching after years of researching numbers and consulting with thousands of clients. It's also my trademark and intellectual property. Numerology, also called the science of numbers, has many schools. I practice the Vedic tradition and find that system to be more accurate. Basic numerology consists of the numbers 1 through 9 and each number is associated with a planet. Number 5, for example, relates to the fast-moving planet Mercury, number 6 carries the energy of Venus, the giver of love and luxury, and number 9 emanates the energy of the hot and energetic Mars. When we combine the energy of numbers and planets and analyze how they interact with one another, we can carry out a better analysis of a person, place, or situation.

As numbers carry planetary energies, they are alive and constantly vibrate when they appear as the address of our home, business, or anywhere else for that matter. Number patching is the technique of adding small numbers to existing numbers with the intention of shifting an existing energy to a more positive one. The numbers added are smaller than the existing numbers to simply shift the energy and not confuse the mailman. I prefer the patch (meaning the extra numbers) to be in yellow or gold.

After coming to America many years ago, I lived in an apartment number 27 in the city of San Leandro in Northern

California. Working various jobs to keep afloat and trying to catch a break, I decided to add the numbers 336 to my door one morning. I did so because these numbers were all compatible with my basic energy and incredibly, my luck changed. This was the first patch I had ever tried and it was my own apartment. Soon after, I met the right people and was able to start my own consulting business. Good things followed and some years passed happily by. I found my first home and felt grateful and blessed.

In early 2000, I was contacted by a radio station in San Francisco to be a guest and talk about the power of numbers. Within a short period of time, many more media and print outlets asked to feature me.

As a licensed broker in the state of California, I was actively pursuing my real estate trade at that time. Callers would ask questions about their homes and the art of number patching became quite popular. I was also able to help many of my clients with their real estate as well as in other areas of their lives.

As an example, let's take someone who was born on May 5, 1970 and lives in a house number 180. This date of birth falls under the earth sign Taurus and is influenced by planet Venus, the number 6. The compound number of this date adds up to a number 27, an aggressive form of Mars energy. The number 180 has Sun (1) and Saturn (8) energy, as well as the energy of 0 which is considered an amplifier. A 0 magnifies the energy of the number or numbers it comes with. In many adverse combinations, like the home number in this example in which the Sun collides with Saturn, the 0 makes the vibration even more undesirable.

Based on this particular date of birth and to match the energy of the compound number, the number 5 representing Mercury energy and the number 6 representing Venus energy would be a good patch. With this addition, the energy would shift to 180 6. The patch (in this case, the number 6), should be yellow or gold in color, smaller than the existing numbers, and placed next to the address on the dwelling. Many times, associations of smaller units are not comfortable with added numbers. In that case, the combination should be placed above the entryway inside.

If there's more than one person living in the home the patch could be different. In some cases, two or three extra numbers should be added depending upon the dates of birth of all occupants of the residence. Patches have been used successfully to sell homes that don't move. Ultimately, patching homes is my second choice. Real estate agents and buyers alike contact me and I always suggest buying a property that has compatible numbers, not buying and patching later. Patches are also corrected if an occupant leaves or a new one comes in. Many people who study numbers and intuitives have tried to copy this technique without realizing how complicated it is. Placing wrong numbers on existing numbers is not a good idea, but that's usually what happens when people do it themselves or are advised by others who don't understand the full scope of number patching.

My technique can be used for businesses, too. All numbers do not work with all businesses. For example, the numbers 2 and 7 work well with the food and beverage business, the number 9 works well with the real estate business, and the number 6 works well with the hotel industry or the media. This information changes with different dates of birth and can become quite complex.

I was invited to visit a client who owned a successful trucking company in California's Central Valley. His trucking company suddenly started to decline and he felt stuck. Upon arriving at the business location, I walked around with my client and made some suggestions with which he agreed. As we walked around his office complex, I noticed that the property number 32 had an extra number taped to it. I asked my client why he had an extra number and he mentioned that one of his previous employees, who claimed to be an expert in numbers, had added that number and soon after, the business started going down. He had answered my question. This business didn't even need a patch and certainly didn't need one. Soon after the erroneous patch was removed and some changes were made, my client's trucking company went back to being a profitable business. Due diligence is necessary before adding any numbers on your properties as a one wrong patch could create unnecessary challenges. Many intuitives copy content from my videos and books and pass it on as their own, not realizing the harm they could create to another person.

Another client called me from Arizona. She lived in a small condo but the numbers on the unit were not flowing with her personal numbers. She was in the process of writing her book when she suddenly became stuck. The patch that she had added to her condominium was incorrect because she didn't fully understand the concept of number patching after reading my book and watching my YouTube videos. After her reading with me, the patch was corrected and her mental block was cleared. She was on her way to completing her book again. Number patching is indeed complex but its results are nothing short of incredible. It amazes me to see what positive shifts patching brings about in my clients' lives.

One of my extended family members insisted on meeting with me during one of my trips to New Delhi. I was invited to her home in a posh neighborhood and although the house was well-decorated, I felt the energy was stagnant. After spending some time in the space, I suggested that the home be patched to invite more Venus energy that would complement the profession of both adults in the house. Things started shifting after the patch and the flow of money increased. I happened to be in New Delhi again in early 2019 and was quite surprised to find out that her residence had been picked up by a mega Bollywood film production house to shoot a portion of a film that featured some of the biggest names in the film industry. I got invited again to watch the shoot and meet the stars. I felt that my guides had led me there to make me realize the power of number patching. This happens all the time. Many of my clients have requested me to teach them number patching but I myself find it hard to teach. I feel it's difficult because it's never the same for two people, just as no two people have the same fingerprint.

I had a client who was a real estate agent on the East Coast call me for a session. She sounded down. After looking at her numbers, I told her that her relationship with her husband was not the best, to which she totally agreed. Her husband a well-qualified engineer who was in the process of getting his new start-up company off the ground. The problem was that he was seriously involved with his sister-in-law, my client's sister. Although he was still married to my client, he had stopped coming home and this left her completely heartbroken. The rift in the family was also interrupting her son's concentration, who was training to be a professional tennis player. I suggested some corrections to the house and my client said she was willing to do whatever it took to improve her situation. Her father was visiting from India and was not aware of what was going on. A month after the house energy was adjusted, my client's estranged husband came home to meet his father-in-law. This surprised my client as she wasn't expecting his visit. Things started improving and with time, the couple worked through their problems. Her son was also elevated to playing the international circuit.

When we feel desperate, we try to seek help from people who don't understand energy work, as was my client's case. Before she started working with me, she worked with another consultant who didn't help her because he didn't know what he was doing. It's important to listen to our inner voice—not our desperation—before working with anyone.

I've known a gentleman from the Pacific Islands for many years. He has a government job and is very hardworking with a positive mindset. He started consulting with me some years ago during an economic recession when he was on the verge of losing his home to the bank. He received a loan modification after consulting with me. I suggested that he patch his single-family home with a number that was compatible with all the members of his family. It worked and he was thrilled to have saved his home.

He later consulted with me when he ran for an election in his workplace and, against all odds, prevailed and won an important position. His home that used to carry the energy of Uranus is now a different energy and the family has prospered ever since the energy was shifted. I've also worked with his sister to shift the energy of her home in Sacramento and help her wayward son join the US Air Force. It gives me great happiness to see my clients succeed. I am always grateful.

A couple who lives in the same city as I do has been consulting with me for years. Both work as engineers in Silicon Valley and are financially abundant. Some years ago during a consultation, the husband indicated that he wanted to quit his job and buy a restaurant that was been offered to him by his friend for a good price. After looking at the energy of the business and my client's birth cycle, I suggested that he stay away from the business as it would not work well for him. The loving wife was a big executive and was keen on helping her husband buy the business by cashing some of her shares. Some time passed and I didn't hear from my clients.

Then one day I received a call from them. They wanted me to come down to the business that they had acquired. Upon arriving at the business, I realized that this was the same business they had discussed with me in an earlier meeting.

They told me that after consulting with me, they still decided to move forward and buy the business but soon realized it was a mistake. Ever since they acquired the business, sales went down and employees quit. The business was running at a loss and my clients needed help. They requested that I help them adjust the energy to be able to sell the business.

I made some suggestions and in a few weeks, the business was sold. I had requested my clients to leave a few specific things for the new owner so that he could proper. After the transaction closed my clients got their money but left nothing for the new owner.

Some months later, they called me again. "Can you please come to our home?" the husband asked. Apparently, my clients listed their house for sale because they wanted to downsize but two offers already fell through.

Again the home was patched and the property energy adjusted. Multiple offers came in and the house sold. My happy clients moved to a smaller house in the same city. However, they still didn't care after I had requested them to leave some items in the house as gratitude for the positive energy. The power of number patching is undeniably powerful in shifting the energy of homes and business alike, but there's another element that's necessary: gratitude. Born into the Sikh religion, I was taught that gratitude, service, and giving are essential to prosper in our lives.

After consulting with me, a San Francisco Bay Area TV station named KRON4 changed its building number from 1001 to 1001552 in January 2006. Business for the station had previously been abysmal but after the patch, the station owner stated that business improved. The station was even able to secure a deal to become a MyNetworkTV affiliate. KRON-TV's programming director, Pat Patton, said that "I can tell you things seem to have improved since the change. Morale is better, people are happier."

Energy can also be shifted through plants and flowers around our dwellings. Numbers that are favorable to one's energy can be placed on hollow wires in one's garden with flowers and vines surrounding them. Planting green plants like jade and basil are great to improve the energy of planet Mercury in the house. Personally, I like the color red because it works for me. Carnelian and hibiscus with red flower are close to my entry door. They always bring me luck. Similarly, plants and flowers that work with the colors associated with your numbers should be a part of your garden. They will lift your energy and attract positive vibes into your lives.

I appreciate every person God sends to me, but there are some who start talking about home numbers to their clients without even understanding how complicated numbers really are. In my opinion, people should stick to their own area of expertise and gifts and not misguide their clients about something they have no knowledge of. Number patching is my trademark, but it has been copied by scores and scores of people around the world. A famous astrologer in the Napa Valley area did just that: she had read my book and started giving half-baked information to all her clients. I wish them the best.

Attracting Energy Using
Crystals and Gemstones

Crystals and gemstones are associated with numbers and they can help to raise and clear our energies as well as balance our chakras.

The first one is Amethyst, a purple crystal that most of us are familiar with because it's widely available. Amethyst represents the crown chakra and is often used by intuitives during readings and while channeling and meditating to receive energies from the other side. It's a great crystal to keep in all corners of your home or business in order to connect the vibration of the space with higher frequencies. It's also worn as a pendant to curb desires for excessive drinking or substance abuse.

Many years ago, one of my regular clients from Northern California requested me to check a huge 30,000 square-foot facility. It was a manufacturing unit that housed all kinds of equipment used for printing that suddenly experienced a downward spiral. As the economy tanked, he was getting very nervous about his business that had been in operation for a long period of time. After walking around the facility and checking its numerology, I suggested that he place large Amethyst crystals in all corners of the building and a larger Amethyst geode behind his desk in his office. He agreed to do as I suggested and by the grace of God, the energy of the unit shifted and his business is alive and thriving today.

Another combination that delivers great results is citrine and pyrite. Placing these stones on or behind a desk or close to the entry point of the space works magically in attracting well-paying clients and keeping the energy flowing.

Clear quartz is also excellent as it works to elevate energies. I have realized that clear quartz works better as a sphere that's kept close to the entry point, hung as crystal balls in the center of the space, or placed in all corners of the interior. Burying clear quartz crystals in the foundation of a home or in the corners outside of a constructed dwelling is helpful in keeping the energy of the space protected and the equity high. Another clear gemstone is the Diamond. This gemstone works well to enhance the energies of planet Venus and the crown chakra. A white sapphire also a clear stone that possesses similar properties. A strong Venus energy is essential for our day-to-day existence not just to get by, but to thrive.

As a licensed real estate broker in the State of California, I've used crystals to help my clients enhance the energies of their properties and live happily and successfully for many years.

The world of gemstones is fascinating. Many of us are familiar with their powers and we wear them to increase luck and joy. Here, I'll give you some of the most popular gemstones that I have experienced in the past with my clients.

Yellow sapphire is a gemstone represented by planet Jupiter and worn by businessmen, actors, politicians, and people who need to strengthen the Jupiter energy in their lives. Being the largest planet, a weak Jupiter can bring many challenges. In the early 1990s, a young man who had just finished high school came to see me. He was accompanied by his father who was quite new to the States, as I was at the time. The young man was very excited as he was picked for *The Big Spin*, a show in Sacramento. His first question to me was, "What would bring me luck in the show?" I remember asking him to wear a yellow sapphire on the index finger of his right hand. The result amazed me after I found out that he had won a million dollars! The yellow sapphire gave him a major opportunity to change his life for the better.

Ruby is another great gem that is worn in gold on the ring finger of the right hand as it represents the energy of the mighty Sun. A strong Sun in one's chart brings leadership qualities and a weak sun makes one powerless and keeps one in the victim mode, constantly taken advantage of by friends, family, and society. A Ruby works well with a yellow sapphire and it's also worn alongside an Emerald in many cases or with a cat's eye. This combination of ruby and yellow sapphire can be seen on the hands of many celebrities and politicians in the Indian subcontinent. It won't work for everyone as these gemstones have to be in harmony with your numbers. Ruby works well with my numbers and I've worn one for many years.

Emeralds work well as pendants or worn on the pinky finger. This gemstone is also widely used by people in the media and business people. It attracts wealth and brings fame and success if it matches one's date of birth.

Blue sapphire is another gemstone that works miraculously if it suits one's energies. It's worn in silver on the middle finger of the right hand, often with an Emerald on the small finger. If they suit your energy, these yield wonderful results. Amitabh Bachchan, a famous Indian film actor, has worn a blue sapphire successfully whereas princess Diana wore a blue sapphire as a wedding ring but faced many challenges because it didn't complement her energy.

The root chakra, also called the Muladhara Chakra, is one's energetic foundation and brings success in life. The gemstone that works with this energy is the red coral. If one is in the real estate business or other Earth-related business, a red coral that represents the planet Mars will provide a booster charge for success. The red coral is often worn with white pearls, Rubies, and yellow sapphire as they all flow together. If one is facing many challenges in their lives, whether they're monetary, personal, or in business, red coral should be considered after a number analysis as it gives inner strength to prevail.

Cat's eye is another gemstone that works wonders on the root chakra. It comes from many parts of the world. It protects one from hidden enemies and brings sudden strokes of lucks. The best ones come from Sri Lanka and can be found in many colors.

Turquoise is another great semi-precious stone that's very popular in many parts of the world. It works well on the 5th chakra, also known as the throat chakra, and is worn as a bracelet or pendant. Personally, I'm very fond of this gem after it came to me in the form of a bracelet many years ago after having moved to America. It balances many planets and heavy energies. Salman Khan, a famous Indian actor, always wears one as a bracelet on his right hand and swears by it. Turquoise is worn with a red coral by the Native American tribes in Arizona. Turquoise is not an expensive stone and it balances the energy of Jupiter, Venus, and the North and South Nodes. It attracts abundance and all those who feel stuck and need to improve their luck and money situation should wear a turquoise as a pendant or a ring in silver.

Another one of my favorites is a Labradorite. It works well on the sacral chakra and the higher chakras. I always feel guided when I wear this gemstone. It's a magical crystal that raises our intuition and attracts positive energies. It works well when placed closed to the entry door.

Emerald is a very powerful gemstone and the best ones come from Colombia in South America. It represents the fast-moving planet Mercury. Mercury means liquid cash good for businessmen and higher education. It's worn in silver in a ring on the pinky finger of the right hand or around the neck to activate the heart chakra. It can also be worn with a blue sapphire or often with a Ruby after a detailed analysis of one's chart. Many years ago, while on a visit to India, a client consulted with me for her daughter who was taking her board exams. My client was very unsure about her daughter because she was an average student and was worried about her grades in the exams. I suggested that she wear an Emerald ring and the results surprised my client. Her daughter scored high enough on her exams to be admitted to a prestigious Delhi college. People in the legal profession also benefit from this gemstone.

Moldavite is a crystal that works at rapid speed to open the heart chakra. Some of my clients have worn this crystal as a pendant and have been able to open their heart chakra and improve their relationships dramatically.

Black tourmaline is another crystal that many of my clients have used successfully. This crystal works well with the root chakra and absorbs all heavy energies. It's the perfect crystal to carry in one's pocket to overcome and prevail in a legal situation. I have one placed next to my computer on my office desk and it's always worked well for me.

I've also used carnelian for many years. It influences the second chakra and the digestive system. A good digestive system is paramount to attract the energy of money. Carnelian is definitely the crystal to improve the digestive tract and the lower chakras.

Crystals collect a lot of energies and they have to be cleared regularly. Placing them in saltwater twice a year releases all heavy energies and recharges these beautiful stones.

Clear quartz crystal balls work magically if placed in a home. They work well if hung on the ceiling inside the house or placed within the foundation of a home that is under construction. I used a combination of nine clear quartz on a few occasions to sell high-end real estate. Red Coral in a gold ring worn along with yellow sapphire or white pearl is a popular combination to attract real estate and wealth. The numerology needs to be checked prior to using this combination. Red coral is used by the Native Americans for good luck along with Turquoise and is given as a gift to the groom by the bride's family in the Himalayan Kingdom for a successful and happy marriage.

The use of gold is highly auspicious and brings luck to the wearer if it works with his or her energy. I myself am fond of wearing gold in the form of a chain that activates my crown chakra and, being a warm metal, protects my aura from heavy energies entering the body. The use of gold also strengthens the energy of planet Jupiter for luck and expansion. Bear in mind that the element of gold does not work with all signs and it's important to consult an expert before wearing gold in any form. The prices of gold have always gone up in a year 4.

The Relationship of Chakras to Numbers and Businesses

Most people know about the seven chakras in the body and their importance in creating success and prosperity in our lives. These seven chakras are represented by different colors and run along the length of our bodies, from the root of the spine to the crown. Chakras are supposed to function at a normal frequency, but depending on the individual they can work at a slower or faster pace and in some cases, they're blocked.

The first chakra is the root chakra. Just like a tree holds itself up with a strong root system, the human body must be grounded with a strong and open root chakra. As the Earth's energy flows into a plant, so does a strong root chakra keep the foundation of a body strong. When the root chakra is functioning properly, money flows with ease and the lower part of the body including the legs and knees stay strong. Body weight remains in control, too.

The root chakra is red in color and represents the energy of planet Mars, associated with the number 9. Like the foundation of a house, it is the base of our inner energies and if not aligned properly, it will create financial blocks and keep one in a state of constant confusion and lack.

This chakra can be balanced by wearing 6 mukhi, 8 mukhi, 14 mukhi, or 18 mukhi rudraksha beads. They empower the human body to remain strong and overcome all challenges and create a constant flow of income that's necessary to lead a stress-free life.

All Earth-related businesses are connected with this chakra. As a real estate broker in the state of California for many years, I'm happy to report that soon after I started to work on my root chakra with the right remedies, the energy of my real estate business changed gears. Money is attracted to a well-balanced root chakra.

The second chakra sits right below the navel and is the center of our creativity and sensuality. The color of this chakra is orange. Many years ago, after I came to America, I attended a meditation session in Berkeley and was told that my second chakra needed help. It took me some years to figure out the right ways to fix it. After wearing 2, 10, and 16 faceted rudraksha beads, the chakra was cleared and my creative projects moved at a faster pace. Issues with debt and legal trouble are also removed by opening this chakra. Creativity and digestion are improved too by working on this chakra. I personally believe that a good digestive system is linked to our money-making abilities. Keeping the second chakra clear, therefore, is very important.

The third chakra is located just above the navel area is also a very important energy center. It provides us with all the necessities of life and helps us face life challenges without fear, thereby enhancing our confidence levels. This chakra can be strengthened by wearing a ruby in a gold ring or specific rudraksha beads after a detailed birth chart analysis has been performed. This is an important chakra for initiating. I have a client who works for a company that does electrical projects for large companies. His wife often used to complain that he was out of work for long periods. On my suggestion, he wore a 12 mukhi rudraksha bead to activate his third chakra. The energy shifted and he has never been without work since. This chakra also attracts fame and keeps one moving on his life path.

The fourth chakra is the heart chakra, our center for unconditional love and manifestation. Personal relationships and the power of manifestation can be improved by working on this chakra. Wearing 15 mukhi and 19 mukhi rudraksha are very popular in opening this chakra. This is an important chakra for networking and healing the heart. An active heart chakra draws in unexpected opportunities and helps in multitasking and creating solutions for many blocks. The heart chakra is green in color. I met a young lady one time who was a reader and worked with many Hollywood celebrities as their hairdresser. She was facing many personal challenges after divorce. Her second marriage to an art and gem dealer was not doing well. She was adamant on opening her heart chakra and chose to wear a moldavite as a pendant based on her own intuition. He second marriage did not work out either. She sought my consultation, but by then it was too late. I suggested a 19 mukhi rudraksha for clearing and opening the heart chakra. Later on she moved to the East Coast and found stability.

The fifth chakra is the throat chakra that represents our inner voice and is greenish blue in color. It is one of the higher chakras and if disturbed, it will affect the other chakras. Turquoise is a great crystal to wear around the throat chakra. Once activated, it brings luck and abundance. Rudraksha beads also help activate the throat chakra. This is an important chakra for marketing. Wearing a rudraksha with 11 mukhi helps in clearing and activating the throat chakra. The immune system can be improved by working on this chakra.

The sixth chakra is dark blue in color and is also called the third eye. It vibrates with the energy of Aum. Aum is a sacred Sanskrit word and many say that it's the voice of the universe. When activated, this chakra acts like a GPS and always takes one to the right place at the right time. It enhances one's intuition to receive constant messages from the universe. The 17 mukhi rudraksha beads work well to augment this chakra. This chakra keeps one on track so that time is not wasted on trial and error. It also helps to create wealth by lucky circumstances and brilliant ideas that constantly flow to the mind.

The seventh chakra is the crown chakra that connects us to the higher energies of the universe and the heavens. This chakra is very important during meditation and channeling energies. Money is also attracted when this chakra is working at its optimum frequency. Clear quartz, diamonds, and one mukhi rudraksha work well to open this energy. The color of this chakra is white or purple. This color is often used on websites and business cards of successful companies. The energy drawn from the crown chakra is limitless. Many say that money is attracted from the root chakra and the crown chakra, so it's crucial to keep these chakras balanced and cleared at all times.

The seven chakras are further divided into physical, emotional and mental chakras. The first and second chakras are the physical chakras and their colors are red and orange. The third and fourth chakras are the emotional chakras and their colors are yellow and green. The fifth, sixth, and seventh chakras are the mental chakras and their colors greenish blue, indigo blue, and violet. Let's look at how to use the colors of the chakras to our advantage.

Let's say you need to design your business cards. It's a good idea to pick one color each from the physical, mental, and emotional chakras to attract the right energies. The best color combinations would be orange, green, and blue or red, yellow, and violet. These are just examples, but color matches can be made according to one's own numerology. Colors can also be used for finding the right color car or the right shade of paint for a home to attract luck, success, and abundance.

The rudraksha beads that I personally like are the 14 faceted and 19 faceted rudraksha beads. The 14 faceted rudraksha beads work on the third eye and balance the energy of the root chakra as well. The 14 mukhi rudraksha is also good to remove energies that are heavy on the mind and soul. One of my clients who constantly had nightmares and low self-esteem benefitted immensely by wearing the 14 mukhi rudraksha. She was finally able to release herself from difficult relationships and focus on her career and education. Nightmares didn't bother her anymore. The 19 mukhi rudraksha is great for the heart chakra and to enhance the power of manifestation. There are many other rudraksha beads that should be worn after consulting with experts in the field of energy.

The rudraksha beads carry energy and are very mysterious. I have had clients who lost them suddenly and wondered why that happened. I have experienced this myself but I feel blessed and grateful to have worked with them.

Many people often get confused in deciding which rudraksha beads to wear. I've had a young lady and her mother as my clients for a while. The daughter was working for a prestigious company in the San Francisco Bay Area. She and her mother came to see me one time. The young lady was having a lot of issues and felt possessed by heavier energies. On my suggestion, she wore a 10, 11, and 12 mukhi rudrakshas as a necklace. One morning soon after, her mother called me very disturbed. She said her daughter blanked out while driving to work and crossed a few red lights before the car came to a screeching halt. The mother told me that the cops were surprised that no one was injured and the daughter was safe. I believe she was protected by the energy of the necklace and since then, she has been happy and successful.

Spiritual development is very important to be a successful business person. Many successful business people work on their chakras constantly to make them vibrate at the optimum frequency to attract prosperity and abundance. All chakras are related to certain body glands. An overactive or a underactive chakra will show its effects in many ways including business issues and health problems. The chakras can also be related to our business planning, networking, marketing, vision, and opportunities.

Many techniques are used to work on the chakras from meditating to yoga to wearing gemstones and the appropriate rudraksha beads. There are many sources that sell rudraksha beads. Some of them sell fake beads as well. It is important to work with a genuine source to get the highest and most potent effect from these powerful beads. Clearing spaces, homes, and businesses is very popular these days and is often done remotely with great success.

I have many clients who undergo surgeries for different reasons. Depending on where the person gets operated, the chakras close to the operated areas definitely get affected and have to be cleared. After the chakras are balanced, the recovery becomes easier and faster in my experience. This is a spiritual practice and it highlights the importance of the chakra system in our physical bodies.

I reiterate that money comes from the root chakra or the base chakra. Depending on one's date of birth, a red Coral or a cat's eye can help to open this chakra. An 18 mukhi rudraksha with a 14 mukhi rudraksha are also worn to attract more money into our lives. For those readers, looking for financial stability please do try wearing these beads.

I find it fascinating to deal with medical professionals to improve their business or work on their friends and family to clear heavy energies. One of my clients who is a medical doctor requested me to work with his father to help him heal after his successful spine surgery. The chakra clearing relieved his anxiety and also calmed my client down, who often calls me to clear him while working with many of his patients on a daily basis.

I have an elderly client who often calls me. He is very experienced and has a huge clientele that he consults with in British Columbia, Canada. He tells me that his family members that immigrated from India made it big and are financially abundant. He, on the other hand, lives with his wife and divorced son in a rented home. He is often unhappy when his wife calls him rude words and calls me to get a cleansing. He seems to be interested in my numbers and is constantly researching my work, not realizing that we have different energies. He was wearing an overdose of gems and rudraksha beads that needed to be removed and cleared. Gemstones work only if they vibrate with one's auric frequency. If they don't, they often do not provide the desired results. They also need to be cleared from time to time.

Another one of my clients, was a successful businessman who felt his money energy took a turn for the worse after he bought his wife an expensive diamond ring. He requested me to come to his office and check the energy. It was not his office but the wife's diamond ring that needed to be cleared. She took care of all his accounts and the ring she wore was bringing bad financial energy. Soon after the cleanse, the energy shifted and he was happy with the result. Please do clears gems before using them. They will work wonders for you.

Chakra clearing is extremely important for success, healing, and attracting good energies in our lives. Most people are familiar with clearing spaces using different techniques like burning sage, using salt in various ways, or dowsing spaces to cleanse energies. These methods clear the space but don't clear the chakras, our inner light switches that control outer forces. These switches interact with our aura and the inner energy points that are connected to various glands in our physical bodies. Outer energies enter our bodies from our crown chakra that open up unlimited opportunities. Many of our day-to-day problems are linked to our chakras and can be resolved once the chakras are opened. It's very important to have an open root chakra to attract money into our lives.

CHAPTER THREE

NUMBERS FOR LOVE, HOME, AND BUSINESS

Love Relationships and Numbers

I've met numerous clients over the years who have asked me questions about dating and how they can make it easier for themselves so that they don't waste time on the wrong people and connect with the right energies. Here are my thoughts based on numbers.

Once you know the person's date of birth, you can get an idea of the numbers that are working for that individual and if those numbers are compatible with yours. For example, the number 9 Mars and the number 8 Saturn do not work well together as the planets that represent them have conflicting energies. One of my clients had a daughter who was looking for a match for marriage but was finding it very hard to date a man who had Mars energy. The parents were relentless that the would-be groom was a great catch but each time the process of dating began, the girl found it very hard to understand her date. Some parents push certain partners on their children without realizing the long-term effects of a low vibrational match.

I come from a very traditional family and my parents had a long and happy marriage. I find it difficult to watch young people give up on their relationships and then continue to be unhappy in other relationships. I wish they were more patient and made more serious attempts to stay with their partners. A young client of mine was very upset after her husband told her he wanted to move on. I remember her telling me that she and her husband had taken marriage vows and she didn't understand why he suddenly changed. She was a wonderful young lady who was brought up well by responsible parents.

Name energies are also very important for a successful match even if the dates of birth don't flow well together. The majority of couples may not share the best matching numbers, but in many cases, the compatible name vibration holds them together.

For example, if one has a lot of Sun number 1 energy in their name and their partner has a lot of Uranus number 4 energy, they will make an excellent match. These numbers are mirror images of each other and they connect and hold really well. Jupiter and Mars energies (the numbers 3 and 9, respectively) on name vibrations also hold well as these energies connect together. I have seen compatible name vibrations withstand challenging times. Name vibrations are easier to balance with slight corrections to the spelling of names.

The next important thing to consider is the cycle one is entering. Every year after our birthday, we enter a certain cycle. The planetary alignment shifts and brings a surge of new energy. Let's say that on your birthday you turned 35 and are now entering the 36th year, which means a Mars cycle. The person you are dating will soon be turning 34 and entering the 35th year, a Saturn cycle. With these changing energies, the chances of disagreement rise but you may not understand why you're arguing more often. The energies of Saturn are known for separation, depression, delays, and raising one's blood pressure. Dating under these circumstances would be frustrating, not to mention a waste of time. It is very important, therefore, to keep an eye on your and your partner's changing cycles and make informed decisions.

A couple in British Columbia contacted me about their property and farming business. The wife told me that they had been happily married for many years until the relationship fell apart suddenly and both partners left looking for better relationships. The husband remarried but left his second marriage some years later to come back to his first wife. The wife too was unhappy with her life and decided to give her former husband another chance. I've seen other couples who separated then reunited because the changing energy of their birth cycles made them change their minds; the timing shifted and brought them back together. I have many clients who hit rough patches in their relationships and look for a way out. In my opinion, it's a much better idea to introspect and give yourself and your partner time. Try to understand how the planetary cycles are influencing each of you and adjust until a more favorable time for your relationship returns.

Another important thing that I want to mention is that certain months in a year work for some numbers but not for others. The energies of number 1 work well in the months of July, August or in the early months of the year. The energies of number 3 work well in the months of March, May, October, November, and December. If a number 3 tries to secure a relationship in January, it will prove to be a frustrating attempt and a waste of time.

Say for example that one has a lot of number 1 Sun energy and tries to secure a relationship in the month of April that has a lot of Mars energy. Of course, things will not work as planned. Our numbers work with certain days and months and these factors can be discovered by analyzing a person's date of birth. Knowing one's elements is also very helpful in matching energies. In most cases, earth signs work well with water signs and air signs with fire signs.

Our relationships are related to our chakras that need to be balanced and cleared daily. This can be done by practicing chakra balancing meditations and wearing certain rudraksha beads that keep the chakra energy vibrating at an optimum frequency. As many of us know, seven chakras exist in our auric field. The chakras under our feet are very important as they ground our energies and move earth energy into our bodies. The crown chakra pulls down energy from the heavens and helps to clear stagnant energies from our solar plexus, removing all fear, anger, hurt, pain, grief, and anxiety. The third chakra, also called the power center, must be kept clear to better balance the other chakras. Moving energy through our chakras takes time and practice and should be part of our daily routine. Once energy starts flowing through our chakras, it raises the auric frequency. Our vibration is raised instantly, thereby improving our relationships with people around us. This is why chakra balancing is crucial to attain goals, joy, and personal fulfillment.

Members of the younger generation connect with each other through the internet and different dating sites, yet their quest for the ideal match does not seem to end. They fail to identify the right energies and in the end, they end up without the right partner. I had a young client once who was well-educated and had a good job with the local government. She moved out of her parents' home and started living by herself. She started searching for the right partner but after gaining her newfound freedom, her home became a place for friends to gather and party. She consulted with me on a few occasions regarding possible partners but kept moving between them without settling down with one. After reaching the age of forty and not making any advancements in her love life, she finally decided to move back with her parents. In this case, my client wasted precious time without any result. This behavior seems to be quite common these days and I've noticed this trend consulting with young people. Life is short and time should not be wasted on distractions.

Wearing the right gemstones is very important to attract and balance relationships. Most people love wearing jewelry in the form of gems, crystals, and amulets but wearing the right gems and crystals according to one's own numerology and the couple's energy is equally important. For example, one partner may wear a ruby and the other might wear a blue sapphire. These gemstones oppose each other and are bound to create more discord in the relationship. Other alternatives should be considered to replace these energies with more compatible gemstones. Understanding a small thing like which are the right gems to wear is one of the steps to maintaining love and attraction.

Wearing the right colors per one's numbers is also important to balance one's energies. We use colors in our everyday lives, from our clothing and cars to the paint on our walls and accessories we wear. For example, wearing the color black by someone who has a lot of Mars energy is not a good idea. For someone who has a lot of planet Saturn energy, on the other hand, the color red will not flow well. If one partner wears the color red and the other black, they may bicker or disagree more often.

The seven days of the week also resonate with colors. Monday is the color white, Tuesday the color red, Wednesday green, Thursday yellow, Friday white or light blue, Saturday black, and Sunday red and yellow. Consider carefully the use of colors to keep love and energy flowing between partners.

Colors should also be coordinated in a couple's bedroom. Depending on the energies, there may be a lot of action in the bedroom or too much unhappiness. The colors blue or gold works well in this important area of the house. Sleeping on blue sheets or having a blue comforter is good for the higher chakras and relaxes the mind and creates more happiness. Sleeping with the head pointing in the southern directions also balances energies well. Mirrors in the bedroom are not a good idea and pictures, if any, should be placed on the south wall. Dark colors like red, black, or brown should be avoided in this important area to lead a love-filled life.

The days of the week also correspond to numbers. Monday works well with the numbers 1, 2, and 7. Tuesday rules the number 9 and Wednesday cooperates with the number 5. Numbers 3 and 6 go with Thursday and Friday, respectively. Saturday is linked to the number 8. If you deal with numbers in your work or everyday life, use this information to make informed decisions.

I met a client who was a young lady in her early thirties who came to America and enrolled in college. With time, she earned degrees and completed all technical qualifications to become a nonimmigrant worker contracting with tech companies. This young lady got involved in a love relationship with a coworker and was more focused on trying to resolve her relationship than getting her work done. She would call me for a consultation each time she was heartbroken trying to do the wrong thing. After many such experiences, she learned her lesson that trying to date people at work is not a good idea. She was very lucky to get her permanent status in the US despite this experience.

Another young lady from the Indian continent who's divorced has being consulting with me for a while. She is bright and hardworking but could never keep a job because she kept chasing men at work who would report her to Human Resources for her undue advances and get her fired. She works for an energy company now and calls me frequently trying to find a way to get transferred to another location and chase another prospect. Interestingly enough, she pays me for my time but does the opposite of what I tell her.

I also remember an orthopedic surgeon who came to consult with me a few times. He was performing well in his profession but struggling in his relationships. I made some suggestions to him based on his date of birth and home address. He kept insisting that he was looking for a very good-looking woman to be his wife. I reminded him that looks are not as important as substance and suggested that he use his own intuition to find his dream girl. Like the doctor, many people I meet are academically qualified but spiritually stagnant.

I have consulted with many clients who have great numbers and live and work in compatible number energies. However, they often feel blocked and don't know what to do to break through. They have energy, but don't know what to do with it. The physical body needs movement constantly. Besides the chakra meditation, exercise, yoga, and other meditations help to open the chakras. Looking inward and opening the chakras is always good idea.

There are many other techniques to work on the inner self, like honest reflection and reciting daily mantras.

The year 2021 (in which this book was published) carries the energy of fast-moving planet Mercury. The energy of this year works well with number 5 and number 8 people and also those born under the signs Capricorn and Virgo. I have a client who lives in the Midwest and has been separated for many years. She's a Capricorn who's been in the dating circuit for a long time and has had many issues in love. I heard from her recently about a relationship she found and was hopeful would work. I know it will because it's her season now and things will fall into place for her at the right time. Each of us is born under a different energy pattern and we all experience luck at different times and intervals. Always remain positive and hopeful. If you haven't yet found the right partner, your season is bound to come. Be patient and gentle on yourself. Practice common sense to find and keep a dedicated person by your side.

Business and Numbers

Different numbers are good for different businesses. The food and beverage industry is governed by the numbers 2 and 7, which are represented by the energy of the Moon and planet Neptune. These numbers play an important part in the success of this type of business.

There are many examples of successful food chains that carry this energy and the one I want to point out is a large and successful food chain spread across America by the name of Safeway.

$$S \quad A \quad F \quad E \quad W \quad A \quad Y$$
$$3+1+8+5+6+1+1 \qquad =25$$

It's May 2020 as I write this chapter, and due to the global pandemic and shelter-in-place order, many food and grocery stores, including Safeway, are open and seem to be even busier than before as people stock up on essentials. The name energy of Safeway carries the vibrations of planet Neptune, represented by the number 7. It also has 7 letters in the name, which is ideal for the food and grocery business.

Sometimes my clients invite me to visit their businesses and I once went to an Indian Restaurant in Menlo Park, California. The owners of this location were struggling to make ends meet, as the restaurant was located on a very busy street with many other food places around it. They eventually listed the business for sale and many prospective buyers went in and out. After inspecting the energy of the place, I suggested that the numbers on the front door be patched to express more Neptune energy. The shift happened quickly and the owners were thrilled to receive a good offer and close the sale. This is the power of matching the energy of this kind of business with the right numbers.

Another client of mine owned a fleet of trucks and became very successful in the trucking business. The city of Fremont was growing fast and many East Indian restaurants were coming up because of a large Indian population in this city. So he and his partners picked a location and built the place from the ground up.

Hoping that the venture would be a success, he used equities from his other properties to fund the new business. When he was almost finished, he invited me to check his new location and provide my input. I wasn't too happy with the name and the address of the business but I also wasn't inclined to scare my client. A few months after opening, the business shut its doors and my hard-working client's investment went down the drain. Due diligence *before* getting into a business is necessary for its long-term success, as is consulting with your advisors at the right time.

Many of my other clients' food business have grown and expanded, including a Thai restaurant in the city of Fremont that has become the best in the city for many years. I'm very happy to see the owners prospering each time I pass that location.

The energies of the Moon and Neptune are responsible for bringing abundance and prosperity in the food and beverage business.

Sports is a big business well known to all of us. Huge amounts of money are made by winning teams and the franchises that own them. I have had the chance to provide consultation in this field in the past. Numbers play an important role on the name of the teams and the players and also the jersey numbers worn by them to gain the winning edge. Colors that correspond with the team numbers and the logos are also very important. Here is an example.

S A N		J O S E		S H A R K S	
3+1+5		1+7+3+5		3+5+1+2+2+3	
9	+	16	+	16	=41

The San Jose Sharks is an ice hockey team based in San Jose, California. Being a local of the Bay Area, I've been following them for many years. Just like the unstable and mercurial number 41 of their name energy, their performance is up and down. The heavy energy of the color black in their logo drags the energy down as it's represented by a cold planet Saturn. I feel that small changes made to the name of the team and minor corrections on the logo would improve the luck of the team.

Another local Bay Area team known as the Oakland Raiders changed its name to the Las Vegas Raiders and relocated to the Las Vegas metropolitan area. The team colors are silver and black. The logo is also black with two daggers piercing a man's head in black. The helmet that carries the logo is worn around the crown chakra, the highest chakra in the human body. Because the color of the chakra is purple, the energy of success is disturbed by the black color of the logo and the symbol it carries. The color black on this team uniform, obviously, is not the best either.

L A S		V E G A S		R A I D E R S	
3+1+3		6+5+3+1+3		2+1+1+4+5+2+3	
7	+	18	+	18	=43

This team's new name is better than their previous name, Oakland Raiders, and is also in sync with the name of their new city, Las Vegas. I strongly feel that the colors and logo need to be changed to enhance the luck of this team based on numbers.

Tom Brady

Tom Brady is an American football quarterback for the Tampa Bay Buccaneers. He spent the first 20 seasons of his career with the New England Patriots, where he was a central contributor of the franchise's dynasty from 2001 to 2019. Let's see what makes him such a successful player:

$$\begin{array}{ccc} \text{T O M} & & \text{B R A D Y} \\ 4+7+4 & & 2+2+1+4+1 \\ 15 & + & 10 \qquad =25 \end{array}$$

$$\begin{array}{l} \text{Date of birth: August 3, 1977} \\ 8+3+1977 \qquad\qquad =35 \end{array}$$

Tom Brady boasts the magical number 25 in his name. On February 7, 2021 his team, the Tampa Bay Buccaneers, won the Super Bowl, giving Tom Brady 7 Super Bowl titles. His jersey number also matches his date of birth and as a Leo, he's ruled by the Sun, which is a 1 energy and brings him fame and success.

Over the years, I've observed that jersey numbers vibrate very powerfully for the players who wear them. These numbers need to be in sync with the players' names and dates of birth so that the player can maximize his potential for success. In India, where there is huge interest in cricket and players also wear player numbers, numerologists are consulted before a player is assigned a number. This is done to make sure that the number assigned vibrates with the player's personal energies. Even in individual sports, like tennis or golf, an athlete's date of birth and publicly known name will either help or hinder the athlete. In June 2005, NFL running back Clinton Portis agreed to pay $18,000 to former Washington Redskins teammate Ifeanyi Ohalete to avoid going to trial. When Portis had been traded to the Redskins by the Denver Broncos in 2004, he wanted jersey number 26, which he had worn for two seasons at Denver. However, Ohalete was already wearing 26 for the Redskins. After discussions, the two players agreed that Ohalete would give Portis the number 26 in exchange for $40,000, and he would wear number 30 instead. Clearly, jersey numbers mean a lot to their wearers!

Real Estate Business

Buying, owning, and selling real estate is a lucrative business if it suits your energy. I say this from experience as a licensed real estate broker in the state of California for many years. I'm grateful to have worked with many clients over the years and help them have large equities in their homes.

I've seen people get into the real estate business at the right times and make significant profits on their deals. I've also seen many who just followed the crowd and invested at the wrong times with disappointing results. This happened because the timing was off and their energy didn't connect with property.

I have also experienced the power of the root chakra in the property business. This chakra is red in color and located at the bottom of the spine. It must be activated in order to gain success in property dealings. Many people wear Rudraksha beads to work on this and others use black tourmaline and tigers' eye to activate their root chakra. Red coral is also used to enhance the energies of the root chakra, but I suggest that this gem be worn only after consulting an expert, as it has an intense Mars energy. Regardless, it's used by many successful people in the property business. I have also seen people wear the combination of blue sapphire and emerald. Again, this should only be done after checking one's chart because both of these gemstones are very intense and can work mysteriously.

The name of the real estate business and its address should also be considered carefully. One of my longtime clients suddenly started feeling nervous after the onset of the global pandemic in early 2020 and wanted to sell his food and liquor store in northern California. He didn't want to higher an agent because he wanted to save that commission.

After three unsuccessful attempts of closing escrow, his wife called me one evening and requested that I visit the store and see what was holding up the sale. It was the creaky entry door and the number that needed to be fixed, that was all. The business sold soon after and I'm happy for my client. Oftentimes, energy gets stuck in broken windows and creaky doors. Please fix them as soon as possible whether they belong to your house or a business.

One other East Indian businessman who lives in Mission Hills, California was in the business of constructing and selling homes, but his assets dwindled after the 2007 downturn. A project that he was working on was halfway complete when this happened. The construction material was being imported from China. After borrowing money from his family, he managed to complete the project but was struggling to make payments. Foreclosure loomed and his nights became sleepless. I had worked with this gentleman on an earlier project some years ago and found him to be stingy and egoist. He hired the best local real estate agent but still wasn't able to close the deal. He called me one morning and asked me to review his project that was up for sale. I declined as I did not want to work with him. The following day, he made his wife call me and I agreed to meet them. The home was overlooking the freeway and too close to it. I told him what needed to be done and what it would cost. "If I do these things, what's the guarantee that the property will be sold?" he asked. "I don't have a guarantee. It's up to you," I replied. He conferred with his wife outside and agreed to do as I had suggested. The house sold within a week to an all-cash out-of-state buyer.

Another family that came to consult with me some years ago owned a ranch in California's Central Valley. They owned the ranch jointly with another partner and were struggling to make payments. After looking at the ranch home, I asked them to make some changes besides shifting the outside numbers. The energy moved tremendously. The daughter got married and both of the sons became gainfully employed. The produce was bringing in adequate money for the family to live comfortably.

As he started to become an important member of the family, the couple's new son-in-law started getting some ideas. The brothers and their new brother-in-law bought a chain of fast food restaurants. The problem was that they had no prior experience in this business. As you can imagine, everything turned upside down quickly. From this example we can learn not to venture out into businesses in which we have no experience. I speak from my experience consulting people when I say that it's better to keep your money in the bank and sleep peacefully at night rather than take unnecessary risks.

The Stock Market

Numbers influence certain stocks during favorable time periods. Cryptocurrencies are on the rise and have become very popular with investors under the current economic conditions of the pandemic.

Personally, I don't have much interest in the stock market, but one stock that seems to be moving fast in the year 2021 is Bitcoin. Let's understand why:

$$B \quad I \quad T \quad C \quad O \quad I \quad N$$
$$2+1+4+3+7+1+5 \qquad =23$$

The number 5 is represented by the fast-moving planet Mercury. It not only moves with great speed but also has fluctuating energy. The number 5 works well with the number 5 energy. Bitcoin as shown above also adds up to a 23, which is reduced to a number 5. The year 2021 will benefit Bitcoin investors. They should be ready for a ride and should pay attention to this stock's peak in order to make a timely profit. This information is based solely on the numbers as I interpret them. As always, no one can guarantee anything in life.

Russell Okung is an American football player born on October 7, 1988. He played football for Oklahoma State University, the Seattle Seahawks, and the Denver Broncos.

In December 2020, Okung decided that he wanted half of his $13,000,000 contract to be paid in Bitcoin. At that time, the price of Bitcoin was $27,000. In March 2021, just over a year later, the price of Bitcoin reached $61,000. This means Okung turned his $13,000,000 salary into over $21,000,000.

$$R \ U \ S \ S \ E \ L \ L \qquad O \ K \ U \ N \ G$$
$$2+6+3+3+5+3+3 \qquad 7+2+6+5+3$$
$$25 \qquad + \qquad 23 \qquad =48$$

$$\text{Date of birth: October 7, 1988}$$
$$10+7+26 \qquad =43$$

The number 7 is an intuitive number and Russell Okung has a 7 in his name, date of birth, and compound number. Ruled by Venus, the number 6, his money luck improved after his 33rd birthday on October 7, 2020. We all go through cycles that either increase or decrease our money energy depending on our dates of birth.

Business Names

The name of a business is paramount for its success. The right numerological vibration raises the vibration for financial gains. It's also important that the owner or the CEO has the right energy that flows with the business. Let's look at one name of a CEO everyone is familiar with:

MARK   ZUCKERBERG

4+1+2+2   7+6+3+2+5+2+2+5+2+3

9   +   37   =46

Date of birth: May 14, 1984

5+14+1984   =41

FACEBOOK

8+1+3+5+2+7+7+2   =35

The numbers in the above name carry the energy of Mars and Sun, which are both fiery planets. The name total adds up to an excellent Sun combination 46. Also notice the number 37 that comes from the family name and further enhances the energy of the Sun, the giver of fame. There have been some issues in the past with this company but this combination gives Mark the strength to overcome challenging situations, like facing the Congress and overcoming difficult questioning. The compound numbers in his date of birth carry the energy of the fast-moving, money-making planet Mercury.

Most numerologists are not very fond of the number 35 as it's a combination of challenging planets. In this case, however, the 41 in the date of birth connects well with the number 35. Also notice that the day of birth is 14. Any other day of birth would not be able to bear the energy of a company name with number 35. The only drawback is that the company name doesn't work well with number 4 Uranus energy. Because of this, the year 2020 brought many challenges for Facebook. As the year came to an end, Facebook was bombarded with multiple antitrust lawsuits, turning the wheel of fortune temporarily against Mark Zuckerberg and Facebook.

Facebook is a global social network that has billions of customers worldwide. The name Facebook has eight letters and carries a name vibration of 35, also Saturn energy that is good for big business. In this case, the owner of Facebook has strong Mercury energy in his date of birth that blends perfectly with the name of his company. Facebook is located in the San Francisco Bay Area at 1 Hacker Way, Menlo Park, California. The number 1 in the street address serves to further compliment the name of the company. The two Os in the name Facebook help to expand its energies.

This energy works with Mark Zuckerberg because of his personal energy. Each of us has a unique number vibration so this example should not be copied blindly. I have known other companies that carried Saturn energy but weren't as fortunate as Facebook.

A P P L E

1+8+8+3+5   =25

Apple is another global company also located in the San Francisco Bay Area at One Infinite Loop, Cupertino, California. Like its competitor Samsung, the name Apple carries the energy of the very intuitive Neptune. Both companies control a huge share in the world market. Number 7, Neptune, and number 1, the Sun, are both compatible energies, making Apple a highly successful global company.

Another global company that has Jupiter energy in its name and is well-known to all is Microsoft. This company is located at 1 Microsoft Way, Redmond, Washington. Notice that the number 1 begins in all of the above addresses.

Yahoo, a well-known search engine with global reach, has very positive Jupiter energy. The two Os should be noted in the name.

Z O O M

7+7+7+4   =25

Zoom, a video conferencing company, also has two Os in its name and came into high demand due the pandemic that swept across the globe in early 2020. The compound number 25 is in sync with the name energy of the word internet that carries Uranus energy.

G O O G L E

3+7+7+3+3+5   =28

The name Google carries the energy of number 28. Just like Apple, it contains the energy of Sun and Neptune in the name and address. The energy of the mighty Sun in the name of this company makes it the largest search engine in the world. It's located at 1600 Amphitheatre Parkway, Mountain View, California, another successful address that starts with the number 1. Like Facebook, Yahoo, and Zoom, the two Os in the name further amplify its already high energy.

T W I T T E R

4+6+1+4+4+5+2   =26

Like Facebook, Twitter has the energy of planet Saturn in its name vibration. It is located at 1355 Market St, Suite 900, San Francisco, California, yet another street address that begins with the number 1. The name of this company clashes with number 900 that happens to be its suite number. It does not surprise me that this social media platform drew the wrath of former President Donald Trump, who sanctioned its functioning with an executive order signed on May 28, 2020. The energies of the year 2020 don't vibrate with Twitter's name vibration and this resulted in a nosedive for the company.

The CEO of a company is the most important person because he's like the captain who steers the ship in the right direction. Therefore, the basic numerology of the CEO must be strong for the company's success. People associated with the company, like the board members and major stockholders, play a very important part based on their own number vibrations.

Mr. Warren Buffet, the great American businessman, has lived in the same home in Omaha, Nebraska for years. The real estate value around of his home has gone up many times because of his presence in the area. Despite this, Mr. Buffet never sold his home and still operates out of the same residence. It's no wonder he is where he is today: he understands luck and energy better than most millionaires.

Sports and Numbers

One pertinent example is of a famous NBA basketball player named Stephen Curry. Stephen Curry was born on March 14, 1988 and plays basketball for the Golden State Warriors. He's a three-time NBA Champion.

CU R R Y
3+6+2+2+1   =14

G O L D E N   S T A T E   W A R R I O R S
3+7+3+4+5+5   3+4+1+4+5   6+1+2+2+1+7+2+3

27   +   17   +   24   =68/14

The popular name is always important. It vibrates the most because it is spoken the most. Most people know Stephen Curry by his last name, which adds up to a 14. He is born on the 14th and the team for which he plays, the Golden State Warriors, also reduces to a number 5. The number 5 works best with another number 5 and because it represents the energy of fast-moving Mercury, this number gives Curry the speed and agility needed on the court. Being a Pisces, Curry is ruled by the largest planet, lucky Jupiter that further enhances his luck. No wonder he's been named the team's most valuable player.

Jeff Bezos, founder and CEO of Amazon, was born on January 12, 1964. Known by this name popularly, Bezos is a Capricorn and is influenced by strong energies of planet Saturn, which is known to bring business success.

$$
\begin{array}{llll}
\text{J E F F} & & \text{B E Z O S} & \\
1+5+8+8 & & 2+5+7+7+3 & \\
22 & + & 24 & =46
\end{array}
$$

$$
\begin{array}{ll}
\text{A M A Z O N} & \\
1+4+1+7+7+5 & =25
\end{array}
$$

The name Jeff Bezos has a very strong Sun energy influence, also seen in the name vibrations of Prince Harry. The name Amazon is in total sync with his name energy and this makes it a very successful company.

Logos and the colors they display also play an important role in improving the name of the business. Logos should match the energy of the business and should work with the colors of the chakras. For example, helmets worn by sports team and the signs and colors they use also enhance the luck of the business. A local San Francisco football team has struggled for many years because they use black on their helmets and signs that don't enhance their playing abilities. Since the helmet is worn close to the crown chakra, colors that balance that chakra like purple, indigo, and blue work well. Gold also supports the higher chakras.

Sports is a huge business in the world today. Sports teams with the right name numbers and players with the right name vibrations and compatible jersey numbers become huge money makers. Serena Williams, a great American tennis player, comes to mind.

$$
\begin{array}{cc}
\text{S E R E N A} & \text{W I L L I A M S} \\
3+5+2+5+5+1 & 6+1+3+3+1+1+4+3 \\
21 \quad + & 22 \qquad =43
\end{array}
$$

Date of birth: September 26, 1981
9+26+1981   =54

Being a Libra, Serena is ruled by the planet Venus. Her popular name Serena carries the energy of number 21, a very powerful and lucky form of the largest planet Jupiter. The total combination of the name adds up to a number 43, a destructive form of Neptune that's perfect to dominate her opponents. The number 54 is her compound number and makes an excellent form of Mars energy that represent success in any enterprise. As in this case, good numbers for sports players translate into great personal and financial success.

Another famous billionaire is Indian businessman Mukesh Ambani, the chairman, managing director, and largest shareholder of Reliance Industries Ltd, a Fortune 500 company and India's most valuable company by market value.

M U K E S H   A M B A N I

4+6+2+5+3+5   1+4+2+1+5+1

25   +   14   =39

Date of birth: April 19, 1957

4+19+1957   =45

The 19 day of birth carries good karma from previous lifetimes. The name energy 39 is a very high vibration of planet Jupiter, the largest planet. The number 45 signals Mars energy that keeps Mr. Ambani's energy rising and flowing at all times. In 2021, he entered his 64th year that matches the energy of 19 in his day of birth. This brings even more luck to him.

The name of his residence is Antilia, one of the most expensive properties in the world. The number vibration of this name is 16, a very mysterious number that carries the energy of Neptune and is in sync with Mr. Ambani's date of birth.

Pets and Numbers

Dogs, cats, birds, and different kinds of reptiles are often kept as pets. In certain Arab countries, tigers, lions, and leopards can also be kept as pets. In the Far East, dogs are more visible in homes as they are considered to be lucky and often attract wealth by blocking energies that are unhealthy or harmful. Dogs are also used for security purposes for guarding various entryways into the home and other crowded spaces and sensing suspicious activity. Autistic, blind, and other special needs persons use dogs for physical assistance and emotional support.

Let's look at some dog breeds and their name numbers:

L A B R A D O R

3+1+2+2+1+4+7+2   =22

GERMAN   SHEPHERD
3+5+2+4+1+5   3+5+5+8+5+5+2+4
    20   +   37   =57

BULLDOG
2+6+3+3+4+7+3   =28

POODLE
8+7+7+4+3+5   =34

GOLDEN   RETRIEVER
3+7+3+4+5+5   2+5+4+2+1+5+6+5+2
    27   +   32   =59

FRENCH   BULLDOG
8+2+5+5+3+5   2+6+3+3+4+7+3
    28   +   28   =56

ROTTWEILER
2+7+4+4+6+5+1+3+5+2   =39

DOBERMANN
4+7+2+5+2+4+1+5+5   =35

```
  P I T        B U L L
  8+1+4        2+6+3+3
    13     +     14      =27


        B O X E R
        2+7+5+5+2      =21
```

The above are some examples of different dog breeds and their number vibrations. These name numbers give us an idea about the character of the breed. The color of the dog also matters as it carries a planetary energy. I have always been drawn to Boxers and German Shepherds. Their numbers match my number 3 energy. My first dog was a Boxer and I was very fond of him.

The French Bulldog is a breed that's rising in popularity. This breed has a lot of well-balanced Sun and Moon energy. The energy of the name Dobermann carries the energy of planet Saturn, the cold planet, so this breed doesn't work with everyone. The name Pitbull carries the energy of number 27, an aggressive form of Mars energy. Exercise caution if you decide to have this breed as a pet. Dates of birth that contain the numbers 5, 8, 4, and 7 should avoid having a Pitbull, while 3 and 6 dates of birth work well with this breed's energy.

A client whom I've known for several years bought his first home in California's Central Valley. He was super excited and as always, consulted with me to get the best vibration possible. A doctor who recently got married, he invited me to his new home to do a walk-through and suggest changes to enhance the house's energy. The home worked out quite well for my client. He and his wife had two sons and my happy client decided to rent the house and move his medical practice to the San Francisco Bay Area.

The property was rented quickly to new tenants. My client moved out but one month later, I received a frantic call from him. He told me that the renters had allowed another member of the family to live with them and this young lady had a python as a pet. The python had slithered out of its enclosure and was nowhere to be found. The tenants who called to tell him this were very worried, as they had violated the terms of the lease. Luckily, the python was found unharmed in a box in the garage and the matter was sorted out. While exotic pets are appealing to some people, it's never a good idea to keep potentially dangerous animals as pets.

Personally, I feel uncomfortable seeing caged birds as pets. Birds are meant to fly freely and for this reason, I feel that locking them up can't bring any luck to the owner. During one of my trips to India, I passed by a shop that sold caged parakeets. I was tempted to buy a few of the parakeets and let them loose as soon as I was out of the shop owner's sight. My driver, who was a local, insisted that this wasn't a good idea as the caged birds had been conditioned to live in a cage and even if they were let out, they wouldn't know how to defend themselves in the wild and would become easy prey for their predators. His response made me think twice, but I still stand by the principle that many of the animals we keep as pets are meant to be free. Good karma is created by being kind and caring not just to other human beings, but to animals, too.

Education and Numbers

The science of numbers can help us in our education. Over the years, I've had opportunities to consult with many young people from their school days up to college and beyond. I also believe that the names of schools and colleges and the cities they're in must be in sync with one's own vibrations to get good grades and excel in all subjects.

I've known one family in particular for many years. The mother worked hard to support her son and daughter, whom I knew since middle school. The son was brilliant and attended a college in the Bay Area. After graduating, he was offered to attend Massachusetts Institute of Technology on the East Coast or Stanford University on the West Coast. Excited and confused at the same time, his mother approached me and asked which of these prestigious and well-known schools was best for her son. I suggested that her son take the offer for Stanford University, as that school worked better for him based on his numbers. As time passed, the young man did extremely well and in the year 2019, earned his PhD from Stanford University. The young man could have attended MIT instead of Stanford, but his numerology worked better for Stanford and his grades and educational success proved that.

My client's daughter, the younger sister of the Stanford graduate, also attended a school in the Bay Area. She struggled to get past high school and later had a choice to attend San Jose State University or San Francisco State University. I suggested that she choose the former but after a tour of the school, the mother and daughter were dissatisfied with the accommodations. So her daughter opted for San Francisco State University instead. A few semesters in, she realized that things were not flowing in her favor. Her grades were dropping and this left her parents very worried. Soon she was forced to drop out and transfer to a university in Hayward, California. This institution worked better for her and she was able to complete her bachelor's degree and is now pursuing her masters in the same university. The example of this young lady showcases the importance of matching our number vibrations with the schools we choose to attend.

Another helpful example is of a young man who came to consult with me in the year 2007. His family owned a transportation business in the San Francisco Bay Area and he was under a lot of pressure from his family members to become a doctor. During our consultation, I told him that he had the numbers to pursue a medical profession and become a doctor. Feeling encouraged, he started to believe my words. He was able to attend a medical college and get his degree. He cleared the USMLE one and two and was later given residency at a hospital in the Central Valley in California. In the meantime, he got married to another medical professional and bought a new house.

I was not aware of his residency in the Central Valley as I had lost touch with him after he completed medical school. I received a call from him one day and he sounded nervous and worried. He told me what was going on and said that he could not pass USMLE three. He was scared that he might not be able to complete his residency.

I quickly identified the block, which happened to be his new home. The energy of the house he had bought was not coinciding with his numbers and was impeding his progress. I made some modifications by patching his house number and later he was able to overcome his hurdles and pass the USMLE three. Our numbers can guide us toward the right career, but we have to believe in our own power and take the necessary steps to manifest the potential of our numerology.

Sometime in late 2018, a client from the East Coast was referred to me by one of my former clients. This young lady called me and sounded very distraught and was in a big hurry to get a reading on her current situation. She was a teacher at a Montessori School in Virginia who was struggling to make ends meet because her husband was not in the best of health. On top of that, both of her grown up sons who lived and worked locally did not want to do anything with their parents. Her house energy was heavy and I suggested that she sell her house and move to a different area in the same state. She agreed and said that she had been getting the same feeling for some time and the house was really disturbing her. Her husband also consulted with me but was not sure if selling the house was the right thing to do. After his wife persisted, the house was listed and after a number patch I suggested, the house was pending sale with a thirty days escrow to close. The husband was dragging his feet and was unsure where to buy the next house. I worked with my clients and soon, a house number 537 that worked well with the energy of the family appeared on the market.

It all worked out by the grace of God. My client quit her job as a teacher at the Montessori School and opened her own Montessori School near her new home. She is very happy and looks to own more schools in the future. Both of her sons now visit regularly and the younger one even moved back in to save some money. She told me that the children who attend her school and their parents are happy. The number 537 carries the energy of Mercury, Jupiter, and Neptune, which are all excellent for the field of education.

I also believe in and have experienced the power of certain gems and crystals to help enhance learning. I've discussed their powers in another chapter of this book. By giving the above examples, I want to highlight the importance of our energies and numbers being in sync to attain success and avoid unnecessary delays in our education.

Autism is sweeping the world and millions of kids are born with this condition. According to *AustismSpeaks.org*, autism has "increased in prevalence by nearly 10 percent, to 1 in 54 children in the US." Truth be told, the school systems are not equipped to handle this. I write this based on my experience with many clients who are struggling with autistic children. As I research more about autism and numbers, one thing I've noticed is that most of these children have good dates of birth. They are very evolved and talented but they're not getting the help they need. I have noticed that the school system is not prepared to help these very complex beings and answers are being sought from everywhere.

Because autism is related to the brain, many brain-based therapies are needed to understand the unique brain function in these children. Besides medical help, the science of numbers can help in harmonizing the energy of these children by correctly adjusting their names to their dates of birth and making their parents aware of what colors work with their numbers. I have known some children who improved with the help of chiropractors and some very intelligent therapists. My advice to parents of autistic children is to constantly ask for help by reaching out of their comfort zone; you will be guided to people who have the right answers for you and your child.

The pandemic that rocked the world in 2020 shut down many business including schools and changed the way education is imparted to children. Remote learning has become the order of the day but many say it's an ineffective way of teaching. It has made learning even more difficult for children with autism. The year 2021 will be a much better year for education, bringing new and improved methods of teaching to repair the struggling education system worldwide.

CHAPTER FOUR

NUMBERS FOR CELEBRITIES AND POLITICS

Numbers for Fame and Celebrities

Numbers and their effects on our day-to-day existence are well known, be it in our personal or business lives. There are many schools of numerology as practiced by the Greeks, Hebrews, Chinese, East Indians, and Western cultures. I have used the Vedic system to decode numbers as I find that system to be more accurate. Over the past twenty years, I have had been fortunate enough to read numbers for thousands of people. Whether it be our romantic, family, friend, or business relationships, the science of numbers makes a profound effect when applied correctly.

Hollywood and Beverly Hills are globally famous destinations. The business of film, television, and the media has a direct relationship with the number 2, which is associated with the intuitive and creative Moon energy. The Number 6, represented by the planet Venus, plays an important role in the glamour business as it's focused on wealth, beauty, passion, fashion, and the arts.

Both the Moon and Venus can also be strengthened by wearing the appropriate gemstones and colors and residing in homes that carry those energies in their addresses. The name Hollywood conveys Neptune energy that flows well with the energies of the Moon and Sun. The Oscars carry the energy of the Sun and take place every year in the month of February, a Uranus number 4 month. I have observed time and time again that titles carrying 1, 2, 4, and 7 energies win the Oscars. In 2020, it was *Parasite*, a film that carries number 7 Neptune vibrations in its title. Film titles too need to be balanced correctly to achieve box office success. Personal names of actors also need to be adjusted to resonate with their individual energies.

Beverly Hills carries the energies of Venus twice and compounds to Jupiter energy, the largest planet that is responsible for expanded luck. It is this name energy that keeps Beverly Hills in a prestigious and wealthy vibration.

Donald Trump

Former President Donald Trump, the 45th President of the United States, has a great combination of numbers. I remember creating a video for YouTube before he was elected to the highest office in the land. His given name carries a lot of Venus energy and this planet represents the number 6. It's all about wealth, beauty, entertainment, luxury and the media for Mr. Trump, who has an overdose of Venus energy that comes through in his quick-witted responses and expressions.

Venus brings strength and vitality in his life. The total name combination of Donald Trump boasts Jupiter energy, the largest and most expansive planet. His date of birth, June 14, 1946, carries a lot of Mercury energy, represented by the number 5. Being a Gemini that is ruled by Mercury gives him great communication skills and also makes his mercurial nature quite evident from his tweets. Some of his tweets have become notorious because they were so direct; that's the Mercury in him. The number 14 in his date of birth matches his energy, but in different way.

This number is great for quick buying and selling and is excellent to make money quickly in business deals. It's a money-making number and Mr. Trump is blessed with all good numbers.

It is also said that one's life and luck depend on one's past life karmas. One can be born as a beggar in the streets or be destined to be the most powerful person on earth. Mr. Trump, therefore, has great past life karma. There is also an influence of Uranus in his compound numbers. Uranus brings the unexpected, enhances intuition, and makes one unconventional in thought and action.

Britney Jean Spears

Britney Jean Spears is an American singer, dancer, and actress. She has appeared frequently in the news for her talent and other personal reasons, including her romantic relationships and business relationship with her father. Are her numbers responsible for making her a household name? Let's take a look:

B R I T N E Y		S P E A R S	
2+2+1+4+5+5+1		3+8+5+1+2+3	
20	+	22	=42

Date of Birth: December 2, 1981

12+2+19	=33

Britney Spears is an excellent example of success in the entertainment business. Being born on the 2nd of December makes her deeply imaginative and creative. She is a Sagittarius ruled by the largest and luckiest planet, Jupiter the number 3. The number 20 appears in her first name as well and the compound vibration of her name number adds up to 42, the perfect number for this kind of career. The compound vibration of her date of birth adds to a master number 33 that is in total sync with her other numbers. She has a career of unending success based on her numbers. This is an excellent example of good karma: all the numbers in the code are well-placed by the Universe.

Jennifer Lawrence

Jennifer Lawrence, the famous Golden Globe and Academy Award-winning actress, who has starred in famous movies like *X-Men*, *Hunger Games*, and *Silver Linings Playbook*, is supported by the energy of planet Venus, number 6. Here is what her birthday spells out:

J E N N I F E R   L A W R E N C E

1+5+5+5+1+8+5+2   3+1+6+2+5+5+3+5

32   +   30   =62

Date of Birth: August 15, 1990

8+15+1990   =42

Her name energy has the number 8 planet, Saturn, that connects well with the number 6 planet, Venus, which shows up on her day of birth and as a compound number. The pattern of planet Venus repeating twice on her numbers brings pure luck, talent, wealth, and good karma. Planet Venus is associated with Friday and white flowers. The only challenge that comes with an overdose of Venus is that love relationships can become a cause of heartache.

As I write this column, I'm drawn to write about the number 4 that is represented by Uranus. The number 4 works well with people or countries that balance it with the number 1 as both are mirror images of one another and complement each other. The number 4 does not work well with the number 6.

Prince Harry and Meghan Markle

Prince Harry and Meghan Markle have been in the news recently and they have some interesting numbers that should be explained:

M E G H A N		M A R K L E	
4+5+3+5+1+5		4+1+2+2+3+5	
23	+	17	=40

P R I N C E		H A R R Y	
8+2+1+5+3+5		5+1+2+2+1	
24	+	11	=35

The name Meghan carries the energy of Mercury and Prince Harry was born under that sign as a Virgo. Her compound energy and her name carry the energy of number 4, represented by Uranus, making her unconventional in her outlook. Just like former President Obama, she is blessed with the combination of the best two energies together, the Sun and Uranus. Meghan Markle was born on August 4, 1981 under the sign of Leo, which is ruled by the number 1. Prince Harry, born on September 15, 1984, is a Virgo, an earth sign, and has the energy of the Sun in his compound numerology. This brings him fame and connects him strongly with the energies of Meghan Markle. However, Prince Harry's name number carries Saturn energy that collides with Meghan's Sun energy. Moreover, being a fire sign, Meghan has the power to burn Prince Harry's earth sign.

Ivanka Trump

I feel drawn to talk about the numerology of Ivanka Trump, Donald Trump's first daughter and former senior adviser to the President of the United States.

I V A N K A	T R U M P	
1+6+1+5+2+1	4+2+6+4+8	
16 +	24	=40

Date of Birth: October 30, 1981

10+30+1981   =59

As we can see, Ivanka Trump was born on October 30, 1981. Her name carries the energy of Neptune and Venus, making her unconventional, intuitive, and spiritual. As a water sign ruled by the planet Mars, she is a good judge of character but can be overly aggressive in her attitude and approach. Her compound number adds up to number five, the energy of quick-moving Mercury. This makes her quick-witted and intelligent, much like her father. She is born on the 30th day, a Jupiter vibration that's expansive and lucky. In the year 2020, she is running her Jupiter cycle. She should be careful when being close to fire as indicated by the energy of Neptune in her first name.

Tom Hanks and Rita Wilson

Tom Hanks and Rita Wilson are both water signs, with Tom being a Cancer and Rita being a Scorpio. They are both led by intuition and creativity. Indeed, anyone who has watched one of their films knows just how creative they are. Let's see just what makes them stay together as well as what separates them in thought and character:

T O M		H A N K S		
4+7+4		5+1+5+2+3		
15	+	16		=31

Date of birth: July 9, 1956

$$7+9+1956 \qquad =37$$

R I T A		W I L S O N		
2+1+4+1		6+1+3+3+7+5		
8	+	25		=33

Date of birth: October 26, 1956

$$10+26+1956 \qquad =57$$

Tom Hanks was born on July 9, 1956. His compound number 37 gives him strong energies emanating from the Sun that make him able to overcome any personal or professional challenge in his life. The unconventional number 31 that makes up Tom's name makes him a loner who's constantly searching in many ways. Number 4 is a mirror image of number 1 and they always complement one another. Cancer is ruled by the energy of the Moon and the number 2 is also a number of creativity. Numbers 1, 2, and 4 are Tom's compatible numbers and so is the year 2020. Tom is in his Sun year currently and his name number and compound numbers are compatible with the energies of number 2020. This is the reason Tom Hanks easily defeated the virus that has spread worldwide.

Rita Wilson was born on October 26, 1956. In the year 2020, both Rita Wilson and Tom Hanks entered their Sun year. Rita's lucky numbers are 1, 3, 5, and 6. She has the energy of planet Jupiter in her compound number that gives her great luck and attracts huge fame and success. Being a Scorpio ruled by number 9, the energy of Mars makes Rita Wilson quite an intense partner.

The Venus energy in her name and the master number 33 give her good fortune and strength to overcome any challenge. The world witnessed a miracle in 2010 as 33 miners who were stuck under the surface of the Earth in Copiapo, Chile were miraculously pulled out alive. That is the strength that Rita Wilson has in her name. Strong, lucky, powerful, and ever protected by her angels because of the number 33.

There are many compatible numbers that keep Tom Hanks and Rita Wilson together. However, the number 9 in Tom's day of birth and the number 26 in Rita's day of birth clash and oppose each other. Like every other couple, they have their fair share of personal challenges that are not made public.

Dalai Lama

The world is familiar with the name Dalai Lama, the Tibetan spiritual leader born as Lhamo Thondup who sought refuge in India after the Chinese annexation of their homeland Tibet in 1962. Since then, the Tibetan community has been given shelter by the Government of India and has spread all over the world. The Dalai Lama travels to many countries regularly and supports organizations and trusts that promote brotherhood and help mankind in various ways. Let's inspect how his name and date of birth encourage his altruistic mission:

$$D \quad A \quad L \quad A \quad I \qquad\qquad L \quad A \quad M \quad A$$
$$4+1+3+1+1 \qquad\qquad 3+1+4+1$$
$$10 \qquad + \qquad 9 \qquad\qquad =19$$

Date of birth: July 6, 1935
$$7+6+1935 \qquad\qquad =31$$

T I B E T

4+1+2+5+4   =16

His popular name, Dalai Lama, carries the energy of the Sun and Mars that combines into number 19 for a strong and persistent energy. People carrying such numbers achieve their goals in life and I feel strongly that Dalai Lama will see a free Tibet. The number 31 in his date of birth makes him unconventional and gives him strong beliefs in his opinions and way of life. The name Tibet, with its number 16, connects completely with all his numbers. Dalai Lama was greatly influenced by Mahatma Gandhi. This does not surprise me at all as they share compatible numbers.

The White House

The White House is the most powerful residence in the world and home to the President of the United States. It has the most celebrated address located at 1600 Pennsylvania Avenue in Washington, D.C.

Looking at the numbers, number 1, represented by the Sun, and number 6, represented by Venus, with two zeros that follow, amplify the energy of the number 1600. This combination emanates the energy of suspicion, distrust, and discord, which is quite evident from the experiences of the occupants who have lived in the White House in the past. This number also carries the energy of loss from storm and fire. The chefs in the White House kitchen should be extra careful while cooking.

T H E		W H I T E		H O U S E	
4+5+5		6+5+1+4+5		5+7+6+3+5	
14	+	21	+	26	=61

On the other hand, the name energy of the White House tallies up to a number 61. This number combination carries the energy of number 6, represented by the planet Venus, and number 1, represented by the mighty Sun. This combination further augments the confusing energy of the number 1600. It's interesting how Donald Trump, who was the 45th President, managed to balance the energy of these numbers, as they're not meant to work well together. The year 2021 doesn't complement the number 1600 or the numbers 61 or 45 either. Many hidden challenges are bound to come up.

The White House has seen it all, from assassinations to impeachments. With all the challenges and difficulties that former Presidents have faced in the White House —including former incumbent President Donald Trump—I, as a numerologist, feel that the energy could be easily corrected by changing the address to 1900. This is a powerful number that would clear negative energies within the White House and make it a much better place for a global leader to live and work. The combination of 1900, with Sun and Mars energies, would melt all the dark and heavy energies for the occupants of the White House, command greater respect from other heads of state, and gain the trust of the American public. The change to 1900 would also be in sync with the number of letters in the White House, which is 10.

Some people reading this suggestion will find this intriguing, and others, absurd and funny. All it takes is the permission of the city and local fire department to turn the 6 into a 9 and change the address (and energy) to 1900 Pennsylvania Avenue, Washington, D.C.

Another famous address is the home of the British Prime Minister, which is 10 Downing Street in London. His current home address has proved lucky for him. The current incumbent, Mr. Boris Johnson, easily defeated the virus that claimed countless lives around the world with his strong home address and his 19 date of birth. This illustrates the power of the Sun, represented by the number 1.

On November 24, 2009, Michaele and Tareq Salahi, a married couple from Virginia, attended a White House state dinner for Indian Prime Minister Manmohan Singh as uninvited guests. Incredibly, they were able to walk through two security checkpoints, enter the White House complex, and meet then-President Barack Obama. This incident resulted in security investigations and legal inquiries, but the Salahis did not get into any trouble.

Former President Obama was in sync with the White House numbers throughout his presidency while former President Trump was been challenged since the day he took office. The number 1 and 4 birthdates have been attracted to the White House in the past.

The current number of the White House does not flow with number 9 Mars energy. This was evident by the swearing in and impeachment of one of its former occupants, Richard Nixon, who was born on January 9, 1913. Mars is aggressive and so was President Nixon. The mysterious number 1600 collided with his numbers and exposed the Watergate scandal that ended his short presidency. Numbers 7 and 9 do not work well and shouldn't be used together in personal numerology as well.

Former President Bill Clinton, born on August 19, 1946, was blessed with Sun energy that was in complete sync with the address of the White House. He too had to face impeachment after his irresponsible personal behavior, but I believe that his strong Sun and number 1 energy saved him from being impeached and allowed him to complete his term in the White House.

Former President Barack Obama was born on August 4, 1961 and became the 44th President of the United States. His numbers had a strong influence of number 1, the Sun, and number 4, Uranus. His numbers were completely in sync with the energies of the White House, which was proven by his comfortable stay and successful completion of two terms despite the accusations made against him.

Former President Donald Trump was born on June 14, 1946 and became the 45th President of the United States. In the year 2020, former President Trump also had to face a vicious opposition that tried to remove him from office by investigating him to the point of impeachment. The influence of Mercury, number 5, helped him overcome all obstacles and keep his presidency.

The number 1600 is also known for deceit and deception. A lot of such energy was reported by the media in the year being 2020 along with various inquiries and investigations conducted during the Trump administration. A pandemic had swept the planet and confusion reigned all over the world. The end of May and June 2020 saw frequent demonstrations by protestors around the White House that forced the former President to be escorted to an underground bunker. Tear gas and rubber bullets had to be used to secure former President Trump's visit to the neighboring St. John's Church, also called the Church of the Presidents. An Army battalion had to be deployed for additional security of the White House. Through it all, former President Trump remained unharmed owing to his strong Mercury energy.

After he entered his Jupiter year as of his birthday in 2020, however, Trump's luck started to change. He entered into a Jupiter year while being ruled by Mercury, and these energies simply don't flow well together. An election he was sure to win suddenly swung the other way. The coming of 2021, a number 5 year, is a fluctuating year that stripped him of the energy needed to win a presidential election. Thousands of his supporters charged up Capitol Hill and ransacked the offices of the US Government. Several lives were lost and the former President was threatened with impeachment in the last two weeks of his presidency. Such is the nature of the very mercurial number 5 that dominates his numbers. This number fluctuates rapidly, causing unprecedented circumstances. This energy is temporary until his birthday in 2021. Things will improve for the former President after he leaves office to plan his next move.

In January 2021, Joe Biden was sworn in as the 46th President of the United States. His numbers are discussed in chapter 8. President Biden will become more successful from the second part of 2021 and onward. The energy of planet Mercury, represented by the number 5, will encourage him to make other changes that will start moving the economy in a positive direction.

U N I T E D	S T A T E S	O F	A M E R I C A
6+5+1+4+5+4	3+4+1+4+5+3	7+8	1+4+5+2+1+3+1
25 +	20 +	15 +	17 =77

As mentioned in an earlier paragraph, the energy of 2021 carries the energy of planet Mercury, the fast-moving planet associated with business, liquidity, and success. The name energy of The United States of America also adds up to a fast-moving Mercury energy. Together, these numbers will be instrumental in moving the economy in a positive direction. By itself, the popular name America adds up to a number 17, a number associated with Saturn. Being a popular name used around the world, the energy of America also complements the energy of planet Mercury. It's meant to be a strong and positive time for America. But the energy of Mercury can also be very slippery. Many political developments will take place that will be out of control due to the energy of 2021. The best way to balance this energy is for our leaders and the government is to keep their word to the people. This will help balance what can otherwise turn into another unstable year.

Kamala Devi Harris is the 49th Vice President of the United States. She is the first female Vice President and the highest-ranking female official in US history. She is also the first African American and Asian American to reach that position. Her popular name, Kamala Harris, creates the energy that vibrates in her favor.

K A M A L A	H A R R I S	
2+1+4+1+3+1	5+1+2+2+1+3	
12 +	14	=26

Date of birth: October 20, 1964

10+20+1964 =50

Vice President Kamala Harris has a strong Mercury influence in her compound numbers that connects completely with her name number, which carries the energy of planet Saturn. She's a successful lawyer and former Attorney General for the State of California. The number 20 in her date of birth makes her very intuitive and connects with 1600, the address of The White House. The year 2021 strengthened her numbers and elevated her to become the first female Vice President of the United States. Currently in her Jupiter year, Kamala's luck will be further enhanced after her birthday in October 2021.

President Joe Biden and Vice President Kamala Harris both share the number 20 in their dates of birth. The inauguration also happened on the 20th of January 2021 and, like I mentioned earlier, the number 1600 is extremely compatible with the number 20.

On March 11, 2021, President Biden signed into law a sweeping $1.9 trillion coronavirus relief package that authorizes federal assistance to help struggling American families and strengthen the US economy. If you add up the numbers of the date on which the law was passed, they equal a 10 (3+11+2021=10). The sum of the relief package, $1.9 trillion, is also a number 10.

President Biden carries the energy of number 1 with him. I'm not surprised that it was he and not his predecessor who was destined to sign the largest relief bill in US history.

CHAPTER FIVE

NUMBER

1

The powerful number 1 is represented by the mighty Sun and is associated with leadership, fame, and success. It vibrates well with numbers 1, 2, and 7 and is opposed by the numbers 3, 6, and 8.

Number 1, the Sun, and number 8, Saturn, are in a state of constant challenge. In Vedic astrology, these two planets are called father and son who never got along. The Sun brings light to the Earth while Saturn is dark and cold. In diplomatic circles, everyone knows about the Is and the Ps. I is represented by number 1 and P is represented by the number 8, per Chaldean numerology. It refers to India and Pakistan in the Asian continent and Israel and Palestine in the Middle East. These countries are always in a state of war that's known to the whole world. As I write this paragraph in June 2020, the tension between India and Pakistan has risen to a flash point that could be disastrous for both countries.

This number appears in our lives on our homes, cars, telephone numbers, and businesses. The number 1 works magically with another 1 in names and businesses. But when number 1 combines with number 3, it's like having two captains on one ship, two strong, opposing energies that both want to lead. I don't like this combination on homes or businesses as it attracts unpredictable situations. I have consulted with many clients who are in a relationship and have the numbers 1 and 3 in their dates of birth. A number 3 person is giving in the relationship and goes out of his or her way to please a number 1 partner. Those ruled by 3 don't hesitate to overspend money to keep their partner content, hoping the 1 will reciprocate. This is seldom the case as the number 1 takes advantage of 3's good and giving heart. They can leave the relationship easily and find other partners without considering the previous relationship. The number 3 take things to heart and often finds it hard to move forward once betrayed.

Number 1 with number 2 can work in two ways. Firstly, 12 will bring hard luck, substance abuse, and loss of wealth. On the other hand, 21 is good for finances, fortune, and success. Very often, a number 1 birthday has a number 2 name vibration and that has worked well. Numbers 1 and 2 represent the Sun and Moon, the yin and yang, and work well together in most cases.

The combination of number 1 and number 6 is not a very desirable energy. Number 16 brings deception, treachery, and loss from fire. Kobe Bryant, the famous NBA basketball player who passed away in early 2020 in a helicopter accident, carried this energy in his name. In home numbers, the combination of 1 and 6 is unfavorable. I have seen people suffer unexpectedly from sickness and losses many times in their lives. Its heavy energy brings health challenges from the waist downwards. Avoid the number 16 if you can.

Numbers 1 and 9 carry the energy of the Sun and Mars, which make it a powerful combination. Prime Minister Boris Johnson is born on June 19, 1964 and displays the power of this combination. He fought back after contracting a deadly virus and regained his health. Such is the power of this combination.

Bill Clinton, also born on a day of the 19th, was a very popular US President. This combination kept him in power and meant nothing could bring him down. His name carried the energies of the Sun as well.

$$\begin{array}{ccc} \text{B I L L} & & \text{C L I N T O N} \\ 2+1+3+3 & & 3+3+1+5+4+7+5 \\ 9 & + & 28 & =37 \end{array}$$

$$\begin{array}{l} \text{Date of birth: August 19, 1946} \\ 8+19+1946 \qquad\qquad =47 \end{array}$$

It is also believed that people who carry the energy of 19 have positive past life karma. Former President Bill Clinton has an auspicious date of birth that indicates good karma in previous lifetimes. This energy helped him get to his high position. His popular name, Bill Clinton, has strong Sun energy, making him famous and unstoppable. His date of birth is also lucky for his wife, Hillary Clinton, as the strong Sun in his name supports the number 26 in her date of birth. The number of his presidency, 42, carried the energy of Venus that kept him in the news for the wrong reasons but worked well for the economy of the United States.

The energies of the Sun are strengthened by wearing gemstones like ruby and use of copper. Elon Musk, the CEO of Tesla and many other businesses, was born on June 28, 1971. He is a water sign as evidenced by his date of birth, making him moody and intuitive. The energies of the powerful Sun in his date of birth and Neptune in his compound numbers are in sync with the company name Tesla, which also carries Neptune energy. His luck works better closer to water. The Tesla manufacturing plant is in the city of Fremont, California in the San Francisco Bay Area, very close to the Pacific Ocean. In June 2020, he entered an unstable Mercury cycle for a year followed by Venus, which will be confusing and make him take wrong decisions that might affect his company. The current Tesla manufacturing plant used to be run by GM for many years but after the last economic slowdown in 2008, it shut down for some time and was later picked up by Elon Musk for his electric car factory. With the current economic slowdown due the global pandemic, Elon will relocate to another state that might not work as well for him. The planet Mercury that he faces as of June 2020 is known for its unpredictable, fast-moving energy. Elon listed all of his real estate holdings in the state of California, which are estimated at $90,000,000, for sale in the month of May 2020.

I've had many clients in the past who have celebrated their 19th birthday. This number carries the luck of another lifetime that makes them successful. However, they can be obstinate and consider themselves better than others. In marriage and relationships, they make difficult partners as they always want to push their points of view on their other half. Most number 1 people have these qualities in general. I have also known many number 1 people who repent making mistakes in relationships and reconnect with past lovers in later years.

I've consulted with many number 1 people over the years. Represented by the rising Sun, people who have this energy can overcome many challenges but often their habit of pushing the envelope puts them on a collision course with the legal system. Number 1 people don't usually win when challenged by the law. My best advice to number 1 people is to pay attention to the karma they are creating or they will have to pay dearly if they overstep their boundaries. The Sun changes signs every four weeks, which also changes its energy.

One of my clients was an MD on the East Coast and consulted with me about her situation. She was depressed after losing her husband, son, and daughter-in-law all in the same year. She told me that her husband, who had a Sun date of birth, insisted to buy a house with a number 13. This was currently her home which she was preparing for sale. Being the patriarch of the house, the family gave in to his demand and difficult times followed for everyone: he lost both of his businesses and their son slipped into depression after his wife passed away in the same home. Most number 1s have the tendency to be headstrong and obstinate at the cost of the wellbeing of their dear ones.

As we know, number energies affect not just people, but entire areas and regions. New York City is also called the financial capital of the world, but there are many other energies that affect this city and its over 8 million residents.

$$\begin{array}{ccc} N\ E\ W & & Y\ O\ R\ K \\ 5+5+6 & & 1+7+2+2 \\ 16 & + & 12 \qquad =28 \end{array}$$

The number 28 adds up to a number 1, but the planets that it represents are the Moon and Saturn, number 2 and 8, respectively. Moon and Saturn are not compatible planets; on the contrary, they make a very dangerous combination. The great city of New York has seen its share of terrorism, including the devastating events of 9/11 that brought down the Twin Towers. Many famous and wealthy people have the number 28 as their date of birth. It's very important to balance one's name energy with compatible numbers. Many people with a 28 date of birth are extremely independent. Women with this date of birth have problems in their relationships because they think like men and use their heads more than their hearts. They are successful in their professional lives but often end up alone in their personal lives.

The famous Indian billionaire Mukesh Ambani was born on the 19th and Tata, an Indian multinational conglomerate, adds up to a number 1. Infosys, a leading tech provider in the global market, also adds up to a number 1 that represents the energy of the mighty Sun.

If the day of your birth is a number 1, consider yourself luckier than most people. The Sun does not hide behind clouds for long and does not fail to bring light to this planet. Just like the

Sun, number 1 people are always visible by their extraordinary words and actions. They are bright like the rising Sun, warm in their approach towards people, and lead by example.

The National Broadcasting Company, along with its cable channels CNBC and MSNBC, is a subsidiary of General Electric. Popularly called NBC, it operates out of New York and matches the energy of the city, making it a successful media company. Let's look at its numbers:

$$\begin{array}{ccc} N & B & C \\ 5+2+3 & & =10 \end{array}$$

The number 10 amplifies the energy of the mighty Sun that brings fame and success. The city of New York, considered by many to be the financial capital of the world, also carries the name energy of the Sun. NBC's vibration is further enhanced by the name energy of New York.

I've had my own experiences with the number 28 and find that it contradicts my energy. I had some close calls during my days of flight instructing while landing at runway 28 in Hayward airport. The front wheel of the airplane exploded soon after touchdown one time, but I was able to control the aircraft and get it off the runway safely.

Another time, my student and I experienced a low-level wind shear while on our final approach to land. I had to take the controls from my student and after two go-arounds, I landed the plane safely. When these events cross my mind, I always remember that the runway number was 28. Although this number proved to be challenging for me, 28 might work great for you depending on your date of birth. Our unique energy determines which numbers challenge or encourage us.

CHAPTER SIX

NUMBER

2

Number 2 is represented by the energies of the Moon and is about creation, intuition, and deception. It matches well with the energy of the Sun, number 1.

The moon moves in cycles, shifting from a new moon to a full moon every 14 days. Many cultures on earth are well aware of the moon's cycles and they use these changes to their advantage. The new moon or rising moon is a good time to start new projects while the full moon is ideal for completion and manifestation. Many people experience mood changes or sleepless nights during a full moon as its energies affect the water content of the body, just as it affects larger bodies of water like the waves of the ocean and tides. I too have the energy of number 29 in my date of birth and my sleep pattern gets disturbed on full moon nights. Despite this, I enjoy being close to large bodies of water and I am always searching for depth.

Number 2 combines well with the numbers 1, 3, 4, and 7. The number 8 does not work well with this number because the energy of the planets representing them don't vibrate well with each other. If one has a 2 date of birth, then entering a number 8 cycle in one's birth chart or a year that adds up to number 8 should be tread with caution. I have known of many people with a number 2 energy who left this world under the influence of an 8 year. If one has an 8 date of birth, all 2 cycles should be carefully watched.

The US dollar carries the energy of a strong master number when reduced to a number 11. It is the strongest and most desired currency worldwide.

$$D \ O \ L \ L \ A \ R$$
$$4+7+3+3+1+2 \qquad =20$$

$$U \ S \qquad \qquad D \ O \ L \ L \ A \ R$$
$$6+3 \qquad + \qquad 4+7+3+3+1+2 \qquad =29$$

The energy of the European currency the euro matches that of the US dollar.

$$E \ U \ R \ O$$
$$5+6+2+7 \qquad =20$$

The energy of the Japanese yen is also energetically close to that of the US dollar and the euro.

$$Y \quad E \quad N$$
$$1+5+5 \qquad =11$$

Number 2 by itself is not a desirable number to have in a home address as it often brings relationship challenges and money issues. White pearl and moonstone work well to strengthen weak moon energies. Silver is also recommended to raise moon vibrations. Monday, traditionally considered the second day of the week and named after the moon, represents the number 2. The numbers 2 and 7 have a magical connection. Most people who carry the energy of these two numbers are very intuitive but often get confused when trying to handle complex situations and ignore their own intuition, looking instead to the outside for answers.

A young lady who consulted with me had the energy of 2 and 7 in her chart. She was separated from her husband and was in the process of legally divorcing. I told her that the energy would turn around for her and that she and her husband would reconcile and give each other another chance. She confessed that she had felt the same way but was seeking confirmation. Intuitively, she already knew the answer. For those who are ruled by the number 2, I urge you to listen to your inner voice as it's always right. The downfall of this number is that it also makes one lazy and fall in love deeply without understanding the other person. The result is often heartbreak. Being dreamy and imaginative makes one idealistic instead of realistic. Number 2 people should train themselves to follow a strict schedule so that they remain in touch with reality. Waking up before the sun rises will also help to keep a positive mindset for number 2 people.

Let's look at one of the top television groups in the United States.

F O X
8+7+5 =20

The Fox Broadcasting Company, popularly called FOX, has 35 stations operating out of Los Angeles, California. The energy of number 2 is highly creative and imaginative and works well with the media. Many famous film and television titles also carry the energy of the imaginative moon. Being a number for creativity, number 2 works wonderfully well for people in the arts and the film and television industry. Many famous celebrities have this energy in their numbers, one example being Michael Jackson. He carried the energy of number 2 in his date of birth and left a tremendous impression on this world with his music.

The number 2 has a great connection with the number 7. The number 27 being a fire sign has also been around me many times in my life, protecting me and bringing me good vibrations. Growing up, I always liked to go out of my way to help people and expected that people would do the same for me. With time, I learned that this isn't true because we meet people who are influenced by number energies that are different from ours. Creating expectations from others is never a good idea, as it leads to disappointment. My life experiences have taught me to expect things from no one but myself.

Being under the energy of number 2 means I've had to teach myself how to maintain a positive mindset through anything. I used to feel moody and depressed in my younger years after leaving my native country and immigrating to America. As beautiful as America is, I still missed my homeland. I often recognize when the Universe has messages for me that I can interpret in order to know what's coming. My dreams guide me, too. Number 2 people need to search for their strengths, as they have many that they may not always recognize.

I've experienced important life changes while living in number 2 homes. In fact, two of the most important ones happened in moon energy homes. I experienced the first shift while living with my maternal grandparents. They lived in the beautiful Doon valley at the foothills of the Himalayas. I cleared my first competitive exam to join the National Defense Academy in India. At that time, I wasn't aware of numbers. But with experience and research, I realized that number patterns that work in our favor repeat themselves often. I had a similar experience living in a number 2 residence right after moving to the United States. I ended up in a small farming town in Northern California that had a sizable Sikh population. Although I wasn't aware of it at that time, the Sikh temple I joined had the energy of number 2. Being a Sikh myself, I was allowed to live on the temple premises for over a month. The head priest started talking to me one evening. Over the course of our conversation, the topic of numbers came in. I happened to say something about the number of his license plate as we were walking by his car. He looked at me and became more curious. He invited me to visit the apartment where he resided and we continued to have such great conversations that one day he invited me to stay there until I could find a place of my own. The head priest even helped me with money (that I later returned, of course) and my life came back on the right track. Soon, I was able to relocate to the Bay Area.

One evening, some years later, while walking around my favorite lake reflecting on my life, I realized that the number 2 address had again worked in my favor. Both times the energy was profound and opened many doors to new opportunities. This is not to say that you should follow my example; what works for me may or may not work for you because every person is under the influence of different number energies.

I can honestly say that the number 2 has helped me. I also like to drive white cars as they work well with my Moon energy and my license plate adds up to a number 2. This also happens to be my second book. The numbers 24 and 33 have been lucky for me in my life path.

Shaun Livingston is a great example of this energy. He benefitted from wearing jersey number 34 while playing basketball for the Golden Gate Warriors (as I mentioned, the numbers 2 and 7 share a magical connection). He was born on September 11, 1985. The compound number for this date of birth is 9+11+1985 = 43.

S H A U N   L I V I N G S T O N

3+5+1+6+5   3+1+6+1+5+3+3+4+7+5

20   +   38   =58

Being a Virgo who's ruled by fast-moving Mercury energy, his pace, agility, and accuracy were all evident on the basketball court. His day of birth is in sync with the energy of Neptune, the number 7. The compound number that adds up to a 43 is a lower shade of Neptune energy, unlike the number 34 I describe in chapter 11. In 2007, while playing for the Los Angeles Clippers against the Charlotte Bobcats, Shaun broke his leg. His inner strength healed him and in the year 2015, he became a key member of the NBA championship team, the Golden State Warriors. His lucky jersey number 34 was in complete sync with his date of birth. Such is the connection between Moon and Neptune. People with number 2 energy in their date of birth should consider the number 7 as a lucky number and vice versa. The connection between these two numbers is like the waves of the ocean that are affected by the phases of the moon. The numbers 2, 4, and 7 are compatible numbers that belong to the same family. These numbers all appeared in Shaun Livingston's number pattern, making him an enlightened and graceful person both on and off the field.

After I started reading numbers on media outlets, some people tried to copy my trademark idea of number patching. One such person started telling her clients to place a number 2 inside their bedroom and above the door to improve struggling relationships.

I found this out from a client who called me from Seattle for a consultation. After looking at her numbers, I gave her the best set of numbers that she needed to use to improve her luck and energy. The number 2 that she had been told to place above her bedroom door was not helping her situation. She removed it, applied the numbers I had suggested, and her relationship finally improved.

Number 2 is a calm, spiritual, and friendly number. Over the years, I have met many talented and successful people with this number who excelled in their fields. Many of them were in the art, film, television, and other creative fields. People with the number 2 in their code should be careful with their investments and stick to what they do best for their own wellbeing.

Mr. Amitabh Bachchan is a well-known movie star who has an 11 date of birth and a huge fan following worldwide. In the early 1990s, his success led him to make some very poor business decisions that forced him to file bankruptcy. He wanted to control the entire Indian movie industry completely but instead fell flat on his face. Later on he focused on his talents and acted only on his strengths, and was able to rise out of a very difficult situation. He is often in the news for the wrong reasons, still making some strange decisions to this day. His moon energy doesn't work well with the number 8, planet Saturn, and to counter that energy he wears a blue sapphire at all times. As I said earlier, number 2 people should be very careful with the number 8's energy. They should completely avoid its energy in their names, home addresses, business names, phone numbers, license plates, and dates with the number 8 in them. Relationships with people who have an 8 date of birth should be considered very carefully to avoid much pain and grief later.

On the other hand, the numbers 2 and 4 have a great relationship and make a positive and successful combination. This combination brings great luck, love, and financial abundance to the right energies. I have noticed this number promoted extensively by many numerologists but just like other numbers, the energy of this number combination will work best if its vibrations flow with you. The combination works well for names and titles used in the film and television business. It's a good idea to consult an expert before you decide to use this number to promote your business.

The number 2 repeating twice makes it a master number 22. The number 2 does not work well with the number 6 and the number 8, i.e., the numbers 26 and 28. The number 22 is not advantageous in a home address, as it creates a lot of confusion for the occupants of the house. White pearl, a number 2 gemstone, is often worn with red coral, a number 9 stone, to create a powerful duo for financial success. Of course, charts need to be analyzed before wearing this combination. These two stones together also work on the root and sacral chakras. They can be worn as pendants and in rings. White pearl is always worn in silver and red coral is worn in gold. Being an Aries ruled by the fiery planet Mars, I wear a white pearl on my pinky finger that keeps me calm and aids in my creativity.

For some cosmic reason, number 2 people falter as business people. They should stick to the creative field and businesses in which they have experience. Number 2 people also make excellent mediators and arbitrators. They are calm, peaceful, impartial, and want the best for everyone.

CHAPTER SEVEN

NUMBER

3

The powerful number 3 is represented by the planet Jupiter and is associated with abundance and all the good things of life. This number represents a steady rise in the life graph from the bottom to the top of the ladder. Many famous celebrities have number 3 as a name vibration and many successful business names and addresses boast its energy.

Number 3 is about spirituality and higher education. This number demands charity and donations to the needy to be successful in life. It works well with the numbers 6 and 9. The numbers 1, 7, and 4 don't vibrate well with its energy. Number 3 people are considered to be lucky as they always will find a way out of challenging situations and an alternate source of money when resources are low. They are good in business and should avoid money making through speculation. Yellow sapphire and amethyst both bring good luck to number 3s. Yellow sapphire worn in a gold ring can be seen on the hand of many famous people to attract expansion and good fortune. Amethyst is worn in silver on the middle finger of the right or left hand.

Sun signs like Pisces and Sagittarius are influenced by this number. All shades of this number like 12, 21, 30, 39, 48, and so on carry the energy of this number. The number 12 is considered to be a hard luck number and it makes one work more for little in return. in home addresses, the number 12 brings money challenges and substance abuse and should be avoided or patched. Similarly, 48 should be avoided in house numbers.

Warren Buffet, the American business tycoon, has the energy of Jupiter in his date of birth. This number encouraged him to work hard from a very young age and keep moving until he reached the top. Tiger Woods, the most well-known American golfer, and LeBron James, the famous basketball superstar, also have this energy in their dates of birth. Famous car companies like BMW carry the energy of Jupiter in their names. Arnold Schwarzenegger, the Hollywood celebrity and former Governor of California, is born on a Jupiter date. Stephen King, the author of famed horror novels that turned into big box office hits like *The Shining* and *The Shawshank Redemption*, also carries the energy of Jupiter.

$$W \ A \ R \ R \ E \ N \qquad B \ U \ F \ F \ E \ T$$
$$6+1+2+2+5+5 \qquad 2+6+8+8+5+4$$
$$21 \qquad + \qquad 33 \qquad =54$$

Date of birth: August 30, 1930
$$8+30+1930 \qquad =51$$

Warren Buffet was born under the sign of Virgo that is ruled by the number 5 and Mercury, a fast-moving planet excellent for business. His numbers are in sync. His name carries the energy of Jupiter and Venus that combines to create a strong combination of Mars energy. Born on a Jupiter day, his date of birth carries the energy of Venus, the creator of wealth and good things in life. As if often the case with those born on a day with 3 energy, Buffet had to work extra hard from a young age to build his way up the ladder. After much sweat, toil, and perseverance, number 3s end up reaching the top in their later years. The numbers 3, 6, and 9 are all compatible numbers and they have blessed Mr. Warren Buffet with a lifetime of success.

$$T\ I\ G\ E\ R \qquad\qquad W\ O\ O\ D\ S$$
$$4+1+3+5+2 \qquad\qquad 6+7+7+4+3$$
$$15 \qquad + \qquad 27 \qquad\qquad =42$$

Date of birth: December 30, 1975
$$12+30+22 \qquad\qquad\qquad =64$$

Tiger Woods was born under the sign of Capricorn which is ruled by the planet Saturn and the number 8. His name number carries the energy of planet Venus that brings him great luck but also many Venus-related problems with the opposite sex. Venus also helps his luck in the game of golf that he's best known for. The word "golf" carries the energy of Jupiter that flows with Woods' date of birth. Born on the 30th, a Jupiter day, his compound number adds up to the powerful number 64, a form of Sun energy seen in the name vibrations of the rich and the famous. His ruler, the planet Saturn number 8, affects him during his Saturn birth cycles. Thus, he is prone to depression due to the influence of the number 8 in his code.

On Tuesday, February 23, 2021, Tiger Woods suffered multiple injuries and underwent surgery after being involved in a single-car rollover accident. He miraculously survived, partly because the date of the incident added up to a number 3.

$$2+23+2021=30$$

Tiger Woods' lucky number 3 saved him once again. Tuesday carries the energy of Mars, the number 9. Woods was born under the sign of Capricorn and is ruled by number 8, so the energy of Mars, the number 9, does not work for him. He has been under the knife several times in the past due to Mars' energy.

The energies of number 3 can be used to strengthen your business and name vibration if they happen to resonate with your date of birth. The color for this number is yellow and the preferred day is Thursday.

$$L\ E\ B\ R\ O\ N \qquad J\ A\ M\ E\ S$$
$$3+5+2+2+7+5 \qquad 1+1+4+5+3$$
$$24 \qquad + \qquad 14 \qquad =38$$

$$\text{Date of birth: December 30, 1984}$$
$$12+30+22 \qquad =64$$

LeBron James was born under the sun sign of Capricorn ruled by planet Saturn that carries the energy of number 8. His popular name, LeBron, has the energy of planet Venus that brings great luck. His compound number 64 carries the energy of the mighty Sun that brings him fame and success and his day of birth on the 30th represents Jupiter energy that is expansive. From the Cleveland Cavaliers to the LA Lakers that won the NBA championship in 2020, LeBron has had a very successful career on the court and in the world of business due to his great numbers. Now, his best days of playing basketball are behind him.

The number 3 opposes the number 1. Every time they come together, the energy changes mysteriously. Their combination is like having two strongheaded captains on one ship. One person who carries the energy of both these numbers is a famous Bollywood star named Sanjay Dutt. His life is an example of how these two numbers can make one experience the highs and lows of fame and success. He has used yellow sapphire and white pearl to balance these conflicting energies and overcome many challenging situations. In many cases, the combination of 1 and 3 makes one very spiritual. This combination wants you to keep giving to help mankind. However, I've also seen many people with the number 13 in their dates of birth who ignore their spiritual calling and never do any charity work. Their energy gets blocked and life becomes an uphill battle. Often they don't understand why. Please keep giving if 13 happens to be your number.

If you were born with a number 3 in your code, consider yourself lucky. Over the years, I have seen relationships between number 1 and number 3 people. Both are strong planets. Number 1 people tend to try to dominate number 3 people, who invariably get taken advantage of. Number 3 people take things to heart and go out of their way to please number 1 people. On the other hand, number 1 people use the situation to their advantage and only work toward their own benefit. Number 1 people like to stay in control and will leave if they feel that things are no longer working to their advantage.

Number 21

Number 21 is a very interesting number and makes for a powerful combination with the Moon and the Sun, the yin and yang energy. One example of this energy is the number 786 which is considered a very auspicious number. It's mentioned in the Holy Quran and is used by a certain community as a good luck charm. Many big production houses use this combination in their businesses to attract huge luck. Many celebrities have a 21 day of birth and have adjusted their name energies to the vibrations of this number to attract success and prosperity.

We all know that the Sun changes houses on the 21st of every month. The summer and winter solstices happen on the 21st of June and 21st of December each year. A 21-faceted rudraksha bead that represents Lord Kubera, the God of wealth, is also ideal to attract wealth and great luck and is used by spiritual as well as business people. Today, we are in the 21st century that has brought huge technological advances like the internet that has connected humankind worldwide. This, again, is the number 21 working its magic.

I've seen many people who live in home numbers 201 or 210 become very prosperous. As always, it's important to know your numbers before you decide to work with this magical number.

Number 12

India has the energy of number 12 in its name. This combination works very differently than the number 21. In home addresses, the number 12 brings financial challenges, monetary loss, and alcohol and substance abuse. If this happens to be your number, please patch it as soon as possible because it brings few positive results and more harm than good.

Number 3 people always find ways to attract money to them. They can multitask to keep the flow of money coming to them. Ruled by the largest planet, Jupiter, the number 3 works well with the energy of gold and gold colors. Former President Donald Trump, who has the energy of Jupiter in his name, is very fond of gold and can be seen in many homes decorated with golden hues. Gold is a warm metal and the color gold is considered to carry the highest vibration. Gold ornaments have been worn by mankind for thousands of years to raise their vibrations to attract wealth and good luck. Number 3 brings great luck when it combines with another number 3, making it the number 33.

Being a number 3 myself and born under the influence of planet Mars, I can tell you from experience that the numbers 4 and 7 are two numbers that never worked with me. Most number 3 people struggle in their younger years then achieve success in later years. They should avoid being too giving and know to protect their energies. I learned in my earlier years that it was not a good idea to give my shirt to someone if it meant I was left out in the cold. This does not mean that number 3s shouldn't do voluntary work or give back in whatever ways they can. They absolutely should, because number 3 people don't have to worry about money. If they stay calm, connected, and in gratitude at all times, money always finds them. I've lived in number 3 cities and always benefitted during my stay there. Years that added up to a number 3 always taught me hard lessons. I have also learned to do social service and give in any form I can; this is very important for number 3 people. Wearing an amethyst, whether in a ring or on a pendant, is a great idea because it opens the crown chakra to draw in unlimited opportunities.

Many consultants tell pregnant mothers to give birth on a number 3 day if the child is being delivered through a C-section. As lucky as the number 3 may be, I don't agree with this because life is ultimately in the hands of the creator.

CHAPTER EIGHT

NUMBER

4

The number 4 is represented by planet Uranus, known to be a very unconventional and rebellious planet. Its energies are similar to planet Saturn and it works in mysterious ways.

People with this energy should take care of their respiratory system. Also, partnerships and speculations with the stock market don't work well with them. They should avoid legal situations at all times or settle them as soon as possible. This number works well with the signs Aquarius and Leo and the numbers 1, 2, and 7.

I met a politician one time who was contemplating running for Congress for a Bay Area district. A friend of mine who knew him well introduced me to him and told him about my knowledge of numbers. A little later, the politician came up to me with our mutual friend to ask about his numbers. His Uranus date of birth pointed to some respiratory challenges and after I mentioned asthma, he was surprised. Looking to our common friend, the politician smiled and asked him if he had told me about his condition. Our friend replied that he didn't even know about his health condition. Fortunately for him, the politician won his reelection as a member of the US Congress. But most number 4s do have issues with the respiratory system.

Number 4 people should avoid litigation at all costs and if they find themselves in a case, they should settle it as soon as possible. I remember meeting the owner of a TV Station in New York in late 2010. After I got off the air, he wanted me to look at his numbers. He had lots of Uranus number 4 energy in his date of birth and name, and I remember telling him to avoid legal situations whenever possible. He looked at me for a few seconds then confessed that he had been involved in a legal battle that dragged for eight years. He said he was adamant to prevail but also admitted that he regretted not settling the case in its initial stages. Like this gentleman, all number 4s should avoid legal matters.

The world today cannot live without the Internet. Let's look at its numbers:

$$I\ N\ T\ E\ R\ N\ E\ T$$
$$1+5+4+5+2+5+5+4\quad =31$$

The planet Uranus rules the name energy of the internet. Uranus is a very unconventional planet and is connected with science and technology. Business names that benefit from the internet have name vibrations that flow with that energy. People who have dates of birth and names that flow with the energy of Uranus are more successful at conducting business related to the internet.

With its Sun energy, Google is the perfect example as the largest search engine on the internet. The Sun energy is the number 1 that rules its name energy and it's in perfect sync with the number 4 of the internet. The combination and attraction of numbers 1 and 4 is magical, even in our personal lives. With their Uranus energy, number 4 people work well with projects that involve science, math, computers, software development, and inventions in biotechnology and computer science.

Number 4 is always drawn to the number 8 mysteriously. It works great with the energy of number 1, represented by Sun. When 1 and 4 come together, the combination is great for quick buying and selling as discussed in chapter 4.

Number 4 brings magical results when combined with number 2. Famous Bollywood actor Mr. Shahrukh Khan has the energy of number 42 in his name and this has made him a superstar. This combination has been used in many TV and film titles to achieve success in ratings and at the box office.

As a name vibration or compound number in a date of birth, 46 brings great luck. But when 4 and 6 combine in a home address, they start to draw in unhealthy relationships like honey draws in bees. I would not recommend the 46 combination on a home number. I have met many people who lived in homes carrying the energy of 4 and 6. This combination attracts outside relationships and leaves the occupants of the residence confused and frustrated. It's important that such a home be patched with the right numbers to shift the energy and bring better vibrations.

Another important aspect I found out about number 4 people is their unconventional nature. They do things in their own ways and still reach their goals. Prince Harry carries the energy of the number 46 in his date of birth and we can see that he's chosen an unconventional path by removing himself from the royal family. Number 4s in medical need should avoid having too many opinions from doctors about their health, as they confuse themselves and can make the wrong decisions.

When the number 4 combines with the number 3, the resulting energy is very destructive. Former President George W. Bush, the 43rd President of the United States, is a good example of this. His term saw the collapse of the World Trade Center and the subsequent Iraq War that permanently destabilized the Middle East.

Former President Barack Obama has the number 4 in his date of birth, as described in chapter 14.

The numbers 4 and 5 together are good for broadcasting, production, and filming, and the combination of numbers 4 and 9 is good for biotech research.

Number 4 is not very well-regarded in countries in the Far East like China, where it is banned on license plates. The year 2020 carried a similar energy and China experienced devastation after the virus that originated in Wuhan spread across the globe and threatened the very existence of mankind.

The energy of names is very important for our success but making name changes can become disastrous if not done correctly. I remember that the Chief Minister of an important Indian state added an initial to his middle name and his vibration shifted to a number 4 energy. This change collided with his date of birth and, within a very short period of time, a sudden change of events cost him his position. That's how tricky the energy of number 4 in a person's name can be if it's not compatible with the rest of his or her code.

Joe Biden

Joseph Robinette Biden Jr. is an American politician and the current President of the United States. Having defeated incumbent Donald Trump in the 2020 United States presidential election, he was inaugurated as the 46th President on January 20, 2021.

President Joe Biden's numbers highlights the compatible relationship between the numbers 1, 2, 4, and 7. His day of birth on the 20th, his first name that adds up to a number 13, being the 46th President, and the 1600 address of the White House are all elements that work together.

J O E		B I D E N	
1+7+5		2+1+4+5+5	
13	+	17	=30

Date of birth: November 20, 1942
11+20+1942   =47

A person's popular name is what vibrates in the universe, so President Biden's popular name numbers are being considered. President Joe Biden has a lot of Jupiter energy in his name numbers. As the largest planet, Jupiter has blessed him throughout his life with high positions in the US government. Also blessed with a powerful Moon, President Biden is a skilled diplomat and makes friends with his adversaries easily. His energies are inclined to help the masses. The numbers 2 and 7 and any of their shades are helpful numbers for him. The address of the White House, 1600, and the number of his presidency, 46, both work in his favor.

President Biden has faced a lot of opposition from President Trump and his supporters for prevailing in what they claimed was an unfair election. Planet Jupiter transited on December 20, 2020, which was not very favorable for Mr. Biden. The date of being sworn in, January 20, 2021, was also not auspicious for him. However, the facts that he turned 78 in November 2020 and entered his Neptune year does help him in many ways.

The future does not look too promising for President Biden after taking office. His health will start to become an issue soon after his birthday in November 2021. He will be turning 79 and entering a Saturn cycle. His date of birth that carries the energy of the Moon doesn't coincide well with planet Saturn, so he will have to watch his health.

Names that carry the energy of 11 twice, in both the first and the last name, rise to success. Life presents them with many opportunities that bring them fame and success. The only drawback with this name vibration is that personal relationships don't work well. Regardless, this is definitely a great vibration to have in one's name if it's in tune with the basic energy of one's date of birth.

The energy of number 4 works well with science and medical research. Blue and green colors enhance its energy. The year 2020, that also carried the energy of a master number, is a difficult number to handle and causes confusion as seen by the spread of the pandemic in that year. I have talked about this number in my first book as well.

C O V I D - 19

3+7+6+1+4+1+9   =31

COVID-19 spread all over the Earth in 2020 and devastated mankind causing millions of deaths and putting the brakes on the global economic system. Every system in every country was affected. The year 2020 adds up to a number 4 and so does the name vibration of COVID-19. Different vaccines have emerged to try and stop the spread but unclear and confusing news is being reported by the media. The year 2021 is neutral to the vibration of this virus but 2022 will contradict the energy of COVID-19. The beginning of 2023 will start shutting the virus down.

One of my clients is a single mother of grown-up children. She read my first book some years ago and has been researching numbers since then. During one of her calls, she talked about her grown-up daughter who had left the house and was now living with her friend. Her daughter's new address was a 4, so it didn't surprise me when my client told me that her daughter was diagnosed with breast cancer. She wants her daughter to move back with her but her daughter refuses to listen to her. I wish her the best for early recovery. It is always good to avoid a Uranus address as I have seen this happen many times in the past.

The number 4 does not work well with the energy of number 15 and 24, as they both carry the energy of planet Venus, the number 6. The year 2020 has amply demonstrated that 4 and 6 don't get along by the events that happened throughout the year. Let's look at those energies:

C H I N A

3+5+1+5+1   =15

F R A N C E

8+2+1+5+3+5   =24

Millions of people across the world got contaminated by the virus that originated in China in 2020. There is not one human being on this Earth who hasn't experienced its affects. Later in the year 2020, France came head-on with the Islamic world after certain acts were committed by people of Muslim origin residing in France. The conflictual relationship between number 4 and numbers 15 and 24 can be pacified to some extent by wearing dark green and blue colors.

CHAPTER NINE

NUMBER

5

The number 5 is represented by Mercury and is associated with speed, intelligence, communication, and fluctuating energies. Its color is green and it doesn't vibrate well with red and brown. It vibrates with all numbers except 2, 7, and 9.

The number 5 has a magical connection with number 8 and that's why the green emerald is worn with a blue sapphire often. This 5 and 8 gemstone combination can be seen on the hands of many celebrities and business people based on their numbers.

This is also the numerological connection between the United States and the United Kingdom. The Mercury number 5 and Saturn number 8 connection keep these two countries together like hand and glove and help them connect at all levels.

In his winning days of playing basketball, famous NBA basketball star Michael Jordan used to wear a jersey number 23 to complement his February 17 date of birth. The energy of Mercury, number 23, gave him the speed and accuracy needed to earn huge honors in that sport.

Number 14 carries the energies of the Sun and Uranus and is a very powerful number. Many famous and wealthy people including former President Donald Trump were born on this date. I have personally experienced the energy of this number and have benefitted from it many times. My office carried the energy of this number one time and business was at an all-time high. Many of my clients to whom I've sold properties as a real estate broker have also benefitted from it. It's very important to understand that the energy of this number is timed and lasts for a period of five years, after which it starts slowing down.

Many years ago, after I started out in Northern California, I met a gentleman who ran an upholstery store and was very interested in the information I was sharing with the world. He wanted to buy a home for himself but was struggling. He drove me around the small city in which we lived and we noticed a number 14 property for sale with an in-law suite. I checked the property for him and by the grace of God, he managed to put some money together for the down payment and was able to buy the house. With time, his luck changed and his financial position improved tremendously. I had also told him not to overstay in this property and move out after five years and rent it, as it would be lucky for the renter who would pay him the rent on time. He forgot this part until one day I found out that he was seriously ill and passed away. The number 14 comes with ups and downs, but it has the power to turn one's luck. This number is an excellent example of timed energy and speculation. If this number happens to be your home number, money will be drawn to you for a period of five years and later on the energy spins downward like a wheel of fortune. This effect can be seen in all Mercury vibrations as this planet is known to be fast-moving yet slippery and fluctuating.

Another client was a Latin lady who found me via the internet watching my YouTube channel. She made time to come down to the Bay Area for a consultation. She was an intuitive herself and worked with many spiritualists in the past. As in the earlier example, she also lived in a home with a timed Mercury energy for many years. Her luck started dwindling after five years of living in that house and she ended up losing her husband, who moved out to California. Her grown children started running her life. They wanted her to be away from her husband and not make up with him, which left her confused and depressed. I told her the reason why the energy had shifted in her residence. Looking back at several events in her life, she agreed with me. I suggested a patch on the residence and the energy started shifting favorably, but her husband still hasn't come back. I sincerely hope that he does, because the energy of Mercury can be truly fast-shifting.

My first book, *The Power of Home Numbers*, was published in 2007 and I actively promoted it on local radio stations in the San Francisco Bay Area and many other media outlets on the East Coast. Many people who read my book were looking for answers that had to be carefully gleaned from the content and some didn't realize that it wasn't a how-to book. A lady called me from New York after reading my book and was grateful for being able to sell her home after patching the address and shifting her home number to a 14. She understood the book's message and so did many other readers. I also have a wealthy investor client who keeps changing his home every few years and always makes a profit from the energy of number 14. Since the book's publication, thousands of homes and businesses around the world have been successfully patched.

The famous actor Aamir Khan has a 14 in his date of birth. He's been known to launch all his films in the month of December because of its strong influence of Saturn energy, which has brought him constant success at the box office. When the energy of Saturn, the number 8, becomes active in the winter season, it works well with the energy of Mercury, the number 5. If you have a 5 date of birth, you should use the beginning and end of the year to launch new projects that attract success and abundance.

The year 2021 acts under the energy of planet Mercury, which is fast-moving, mercurial, but also a little unstable. This is certainly a shift in energy from the previous year that will start the process of regaining financial stability worldwide. Cryptocurrencies will be the new trend and the stock market will perform better than in previous years. The price of metals like silver will be on the rise as silver will be used extensively in many industries. With time, silver will be used more than gold and the prices of gold will swing downward. The shift in the energy will become more profound after the middle of May 2021, when the energy of fast-moving and lucky Mercury will become more pronounced.

Number 5 and number 9 have a very challenging relationship. I have met numerous clients over the years who felt the destabilizing energies whenever these numbers came together. Entering a number 5 cycle with a 9 date of birth, or vice versa, always demands caution. I also advise people who have a number 5 in their dates of birth not to have a number 9 vibration in their name, business, or home address. Similarly, I advise number 9 people to avoid the number 5 at all times.

In chapter 13, I mentioned the name JIO, a business that's part of Reliance Industries owned by an Indian billionaire named Mukesh Ambani. This company makes millions of dollars as a telecom company in the populous country of India, where there is a huge fascination with mobile technology. The name JIO carries the energy of number 9 and as I mentioned, the number 9 and number 5 create a very destabilizing dynamic. That's exactly what happened as 2021 approached: a huge farmer protest against the Indian government for repealing farm laws led to the boycott of JIO products sold by Mr. Ambani's Reliance Industries. The company's stocks plunged as JIO, a number 9 energy, collided with 2021, a number 5 energy. The destruction caused by these two energies always repeats, irrespective of the fact that the people it's affecting are rich or poor.

The Prime Minister of India, Mr. Narendra Modi, has a Saturn date of birth. He got married early in life but the relationship didn't work out, as most early marriages don't for people with Saturn birthdates. After that, Mr. Modi preferred to stay a bachelor. The number 5 has played an important role in his life because of his date of birth.

$$
\begin{array}{ccc}
\text{N A R E N D R A} & \text{M O D I} & \\
5{+}1{+}2{+}5{+}5{+}4{+}2{+}1 & 4{+}7{+}4{+}1 & \\
25 \quad\quad + & 16 & =41
\end{array}
$$

$$
\begin{array}{cc}
\text{Date of birth: September 17, 1950} & \\
9{+}17{+}1950 & =41
\end{array}
$$

Mr. Modi became the 14th Prime Minister of India. This example clearly illustrates the magical connection between number 41 (or 5) and number 17. I believe this combination was created by the divine and those who benefit from it (as Mr. Modi does) are blessed and successful.

Former President Donald Trump has a close relationship with Prime Minister Modi. Both of them conducted huge shows in their respective countries for each other. Mr. Trump has a 14 date of birth and was born in the month of June, which has a strong Mercury influence. The Trump Tower on 5th Ave in New York opened on February 14, 1983. The number 5 always works best with another 5, so it's no surprise that these heads of state were so comfortable with one another.

In fact, former President Trump conferred one of the country's highest military decorations, The Legion of Merit, on Prime Minister Modi. The Legion of Merit is the highest degree of the commander-in-chief and is a prestigious award conferred by the President of the United States on the heads of government of other countries. This is a great example of the attraction between number 5 energies, which will become more pronounced in the later part of December 2021 when the energy of planet Saturn, the number 8, kicks in.

Dubai is a global destination known for its incredible wealth and opulence. Let's look at the name of this country and the currency used in the United Arab Emirates.

D U B A I

4+6+2+1+1   =14

D I R H A M

4+1+2+5+1+4   =17

The name Dubai, a number 14, and the currency dirham, a number 17, are in total sync. It's like wearing the compatible combination of an emerald and a blue sapphire.

The name Dubai has five letters in its name and the numerological vibration adds up to the number 14, which is great for fast money. This number works like a wheel of fortune: it goes up quite quickly but then comes down at the same pace. Being timed energy, it should be used quickly before the energy starts drying out. The year 2021 will be a better year for Dubai as its name number matches the number of the year and this will make the energy shift positively.

Kangana Ranaut is a well-known East Indian Bollywood actress who has won many national awards for her acting and films. She was born on March 23, 1987. She overcame many challenges in her life and gained huge fame and success. She was in the news in 2020 after the Maharashtra government in India bulldozed her office building, which was a number 5. The local government was so irate with her for being honest and speaking her mind that they threatened to demolish her residence located on the 5th floor in a posh neighborhood in Mumbai.

This case highlights the number 5: Kangana was born on a day of 23 and this is the reason she chose both her home and office to have Mercury energy. That is a great idea for rising rapidly in a short period of time but like I said earlier, the energy tumbles down just as rapidly. Since the incident in 2020, she left Mumbai to operate from a different location. As you can see, the number 5 is mercurial so please be aware of its energies while working with it. Its energy changes suddenly and unexpectedly.

The year 2021 also carries the energy of the fast-moving planet Mercury. Countries that carry the energy of planet Mars, the number 9, will need to be cautious in their dealings with other countries this year. These are times when they can be destabilized due to the colliding planets. One such country is Iran. The reason Iran and the US have not been able to resume diplomatic relations is because their name numbers clash. The full name of the US adds up to a number 77 (calculated in chapter 4) that opposes the number 9 in Iran. This is the primary reason for the distrust and disagreements that exist between the US and Iran. Based on their numbers, 2021 could even lead to a military clash between these two countries.

$$I \quad R \quad A \quad N$$
$$1+2+1+5 \qquad =9$$

On the other hand, Iran's archrival Iraq will flow much better with the energy 2021 as its name number adds up to a 5.

$$I \quad R \quad A \quad Q$$
$$1+2+1+1 \qquad =5$$

The world knows that Iran, the number 9, and Iraq, the number 5, are such bitter enemies. Numbers don't lie.

CHAPTER TEN

NUMBER

6

The number 6 is connected with the planet Venus and represents wealth, luxury, beauty, arts, money, and the most desired elements of life. Lighter colors like white and cream work well to heighten its energies. It has a magical connection with the intuitive number 2, represented by the Moon, to promote the film and television industry. Number 6 is a highly favored number as it represents the blue sky. Most people like to work with the energy of number 6 due to its immense benefits. Many famous singers, athletes, actors, media personalities, and designers carry the energy of number 6. This number always attracts love and money.

Many businesses carry the energy of Venus in their names and have become immensely successful because of it. Most of us are familiar with a company called My Pillow that has grown in popularity in the United States over the years. The owner of the company was a former drug addict who recovered and made wonders happen by employing thousands of people to work for his company, contributing to the economy, and making an excellent product. The owner of the company has met with former President Donald Trump on many occasions, who also happens to carry the energy of Venus in his name.

$$M \ Y \qquad\qquad P \ I \ L \ L \ O \ W$$
$$4+1 \qquad\qquad 8+1+3+3+7+6$$
$$5 \qquad + \qquad 28 \qquad =33$$

The current speaker of the, House Nancy Pelosi, is another prominent figure who carries Venus' energy in her name. She lives in San Francisco, also a Venus city. I wasn't surprised to see her tear apart Trump's speech after his State of the Union address in 2020. She's an Aries woman ruled by the powerful planet Mars, after all, and is extremely powerful in her party. Luck has been on her side for many years and her love for expensive items is well-known.

$$N \ A \ N \ C \ Y \qquad\qquad P \ E \ L \ O \ S \ I$$
$$5+1+5+3+1 \qquad\qquad 8+5+3+7+3+1$$
$$15 \qquad + \qquad 27 \qquad =42$$

Mrs. Pelosi loves to show the world the ice cream varieties stocked in her refrigerator. Sugar in any form in also Venus energy.

The number 6 appears in home addresses and business names. It's a favored number in the name vibration of many film titles. Some superstars have the energy of this number repeat twice on their names. One example is a famous Indian pop singer who was raised in the family of hymn singing. In the early 90s, his family owned a car service business in Berkeley, California and he supported himself selling burgers as well. Being a talented singer, decided to try his luck in the Indian film industry. Luckily for him, his new name carried the energy of Venus. Today he is known the world over for his music and songs. His name is Daler Mehndi and he illustrates the power of Venus, the number 6, if it works for you.

$$D \; A \; L \; E \; R \qquad M \; E \; H \; N \; D \; I$$
$$4+1+3+5+2 \qquad 4+5+5+5+4+1$$
$$15 \qquad + \qquad 24 \qquad =39$$

As you can see, the energy of planet Venus repeats in the first and the last name of this celebrity, then combines into a very powerful 39. I know some other famous people that carry similar energy. If one has the talent and wants to excel in the entertainment industry (provided the date of birth vibrates with one's energy) such combinations that involve planet Venus should be considered.

Another celebrity by the name of Shahrukh Khan carries a similar energy in his name. He's a global star with a worldwide following. Dubbed "the king of romance," all his films are blockbusters.

$$S \; H \; A \; H \; R \; U \; K \; H \qquad K \; H \; A \; N$$
$$3+5+1+5+2+6+2+5 \qquad 2+5+1+5$$
$$29 \qquad + \qquad 13 \qquad =42$$

Unfortunately, the year 2020 didn't work well with his number 6 vibration. Mr. Khan faced several challenges last year and may face more this year, as his Mars energy will collide with 2021. Numbers don't lie and every human, whether they are young or old, rich or poor, is always tested by the Universe by changing number cycles.

Number 6 is in tune with the numbers 3 and 9, but it doesn't flow well with the numbers 1, 4, and 7. China, which has the energy of number 15, was jolted in the year 2020. Numbers 4 and 8 don't combine well with the number 15. Combined with the number 1, number 6 brings surprises and deception and combined with the number 7, it heralds unknown challenges.

I've known a certain family for many years. Both husband and wife have worked really hard to provide the best for their family members. They consult me once in a while. In a recent reading, the parents told me that their 31-year-old son suddenly decided to leave the house and live with his friends. I understood why, as the home number was 492 and the year was 2020; his numbers took him out. After the mother gave me his new address, I told her that the move to the house with his friends was still not the best idea. The adamant parents are trying very hard to bring him back to their house, but I know it won't happen. The parents wanted me to talk to their son and convince him to return, to which I disagreed. I don't force my advice on anyone because I believe each one of us has to experience life through his or her free will. If he ever needs my advice, the universe will send him to me.

Everyone who lives in the United States knows of an agency called the IRS. This agency, unsurprisingly, also carries the energy of planet Venus. The IRS collects money from people in the form of taxes, demonstrating the power of Venus to hold money.

The reason people wear white gemstones like diamonds, white sapphires, or opals is so that they can improve the vibrational energy of planet Venus and attract beauty and money into their lives. In Vedic tradition, Friday rules the energy of Venus and is considered auspicious for business and money matters. Donations to appease the Goddess Laxmi are made on Fridays by East Indian people around the world. It is believed that by doing so, one will be prosperous and lucky.

Cars and luxury are dominated by the number 6. Driving a white car is considered lucky if Venus flows with one's date of birth. I believe that driving the right color car is imperative for luck and business. Many famous and wealthy people drive white or off-white cars to increase prosperity. Mr. Mukesh Ambani, one of the wealthiest men, is often seen in his white BMW. Since Venus rules luxury, cars are connected to the energy of planet Venus. Porsche and its price tag do not surprise me.

$$P \quad O \quad R \quad S \quad C \quad H \quad E$$
$$8+7+2+3+3+5+5 \quad =33$$

As you can see, the name Porsche carries the energy of a master number 33 that has the energy of planet Jupiter twice. I cover this topic more in chapter 14.

The cities of San Francisco and Paris are brimming with beauty and wealth and are a destination for lovers from around the world. They're also known for high-end fashion and famous tourist attractions like the Golden Gate Bridge and Eiffel Tower. These and many more famous monuments are connected to Venus energy.

Too much Venus energy can bring many personal challenges in people's lives. I have a client whom I've known for many years. She is tall, beautiful, and financially abundant but divorced with constant relationships issues. She's acted in some films as well but can never hold on to a relationship, always suffering with the matters of the heart. Venus does bring such challenges. She often consults with me but still does what she wants to do until she later returns with a broken heart. Her Venus energy is so strong that she chases the men she desires even after the relationship is over hoping for a miracle that hasn't happened until yet. In our last meeting, she showed me the endless number of rings and pendants she had gotten, beautiful and expensive pieces she acquired to attract the love of her life.

Also a master number, 33 is a very lucky number if it works with one's numerology. I've written about it in this book in chapter

14. I've known many people who have the energy of number 33 in their names and easily overcome difficult challenges and have attained great fame. Many businesses that carry this energy in their names are very successful.

Another number that carries the energy of Uranus and Moon is the number 42. The economy flourished when President Bill Clinton, the 42 President of the United States, was in office, clearly demonstrating the money power of Venus energy.

It is important to understand that one shoe does not fit every foot and that the energies of planet Venus don't flow with everyone. Please check your number compatibility before you choose the number 6 to start working for you.

The energy of 2020 has devastated the film production industry in Mumbai, which is ruled by the planet Venus. Drug abuse was found to be a big reason and the media, also ruled by planet Venus, did not leave any stone unturned in their investigations. The biggest celebrities are being questioned and many have been incarcerated. I believe the reason this is happening now is because the energy of the year 2020 and the number 6 (Venus that rules the film and media industry) don't cooperate well together.

The number 24 is also a popular vibration of the planet Venus. Many consider 6 to be the luckiest number. One downfall of number 6 people is that they fall in love without thinking and experience numerous heartbreaks throughout their lives. My advice for numbers 6s is to think more logically and less romantically before making any decisions in love, for their own peace of mind.

Number 51 is not a number I'm fond of. It does add up to a number 6, but number 5 preceding number1 brings many challenges. It makes for a difficult combination on home numbers. Its energy is much like Area 51 in the Nevada mountains: enigmatic and unpredictable. I've spoken about this number in my previous book as well.

CHAPTER ELEVEN

NUMBER

7

Represented by Neptune, number 7 is a magical and mystical number that represents the water of the Earth. It is associated with spirituality and big business names. Its energies work well close to water, such as rivers or ocean. Number 7 has a magical connection with the number 2 represented by the Moon. It does not vibrate well with the numbers 8 and 9, 5 and 6.

This number can appear in our lives in many ways. Gamblers know that the numbers 77 or 777 can suddenly bring money. Personally, I do not gamble or ask anyone to gamble, as life is about sincere effort rather than taking shortcuts. Number 7 also works well in the food and beverage business and in film and photography.

When number 7 combines with the energies of number 1, the Sun, it attracts fame. Numbers 2 and 7 work well with people born under the influence of Mars. With number 3, the number 7 brings great business partnerships. This number has appeared as a jersey number for many famous soccer, football, and basketball players.

Cat's eye is the gemstone that is most compatible with the energies of number 7. People born under the influence of this number need to control their thoughts as they can become erratic in their thinking. Mind calming exercises like yoga and meditation are helpful. Cat's eye works well on the root chakra and protects one from hidden enemies. It is worn by many successful business people across the globe to attract the mysterious energies of wealth to them.

A P P L E

1+8+8+3+5   =25

S A M S U N G

3+1+4+3+6+5+3   =25

Apple and Samsung are two global companies that carry the energies of Neptune in their name. We all know these companies produce tech gadgets that are widely used, but the numbers 7 and 6 do not work together. As I write this page in April 2020, COVID-19 has bought the world to a standstill. I am not surprised to hear that both of these companies have decided to move their operation from China—the country in which COVID-19 originated and a country under the energy of number 6—to other parts of the world.

One of my clients whom I have known for many years is a spiritual worker and well-connected to the Hollywood scene. I remember her first reading with me when I noticed the Moon energy on her date of birth. She was struggling and was in the process of losing her properties due to the economic meltdown. Her home number was not working for her. I suggested that she find a number 25 or 34 on her residence and move from her current location. By the grace of God, she found an apartment with the number 34 in an upscale building in the Los Angeles area.

I got a chance to meet her once and she told me her whole life had changed. She became very busy with her work and her contact with famous people expanded. Her financial situation and reach improved beyond her expectations. This is what one can expect under the magical connection of numbers 2 and 7. These two numbers, like the Moon and rising tides, work in symbiosis for positive change.

Many years ago, I hired a young lady as my personal assistant. Her dad had been my client and he felt that she would be a great fit for my business. I took the chance and she helped me for many years and I will always be grateful to her. During her employment, I helped her and her husband get approved for a loan to buy their first property in the San Francisco Bay Area. It was a single-family home with a number 16. The number matched her name energy but did not work well with her husband and his family. There was constant friction in the house and one day she told me that the house needed some help. After looking at her husband's and his family's energy, I patched the single-family home. The energy shifted and she and her family still live there, now more harmoniously. It's been close to 25 years and the equity in the property has gone up tremendously. I am so happy for her. Her house has the number 16, a very difficult number to handle that invites deception and health challenges that happen on the lower part of the body. If this happens to be your home number, do patch it with a vibration suitable to you.

The seven chakras in the human body and the seven colors of the rainbow are known to all of us. Our chakras are our inner drivers and it is important that they remain balanced and vibrate at a natural pace. There are many ways that the 7 chakras can be balanced to bring the rainbow effect in our lives.

The number 7 is very important for the success of the food and beverage business as well. Number 7 people are good cooks and will be successful in running food businesses close to bodies of water. They should also be careful of the kitchen stove as they often burn themselves. Photography also comes naturally to number 7 people and they often excel in this trade as well as in the film and television business.

Let me give you two examples of this number when it appears as the name of a food business. We've all heard of a fast-food chain called McDonald's. But let's take a closer look at its number vibrations.

$$\text{M c D O N A L D 'S}$$
$$4+3+4+7+5+1+3+4+3 \quad =34$$

This name is known all over the globe with nearly 40,000 franchises worldwide. Many say that it owns the best prime properties in the world and selling fast-food is an add on. The energy of number 34 is a high-vibrating shade of number 7 and is ideal for the food business. McDonald's success definitely lies in its numbers. Had the name combination added up to a number 43 instead, it would have not worked as well because the number 4 (Uranus) before the number 3 (Jupiter) becomes a destructive energy.

The second example is a food chain that is well known in the Northern Hemisphere by the name of Safeway. All those who live in this part of the world know this store well. Let's look at its numbers.

$$\text{S A F E W A Y}$$
$$3+1+8+5+6+1+1 \quad =25$$

This food chain also carries the energy of one shade of Neptune energy. It works quite well for this kind of business but is a few notches lower than the previous example.

Another name known all over the world is Hollywood. But this celebrity city carries the energy of number 43, which is not a very desirable energy. The number brings strife and destruction in many forms. I have met young people who moved to Hollywood from many parts of the world to fulfill their dreams and worked tirelessly but still did not make it. This is the rather unfortunate power of number 43. America had to face many challenges under the 43rd president, including 9/11 and the Iraq war. I have seen this name on homes and businesses of many of my clients and always suggested a patch to pacify the energy.

The number 7 is also considered lucky by many singers and musicians. The world-famous ghazal singer Jagjit Singh always sat in a group of 7 musicians in all his concerts and recordings. His name and music got even bigger after his passing. Casinos all over the world are very fond of the number 7 and they appear as winning numbers or combinations on various gambling machines. On a personal note, I feel that the number 77 carries more luck than 777.

Mahindra Singh Dhoni is an ace cricketer who captained India on to win two World Cups. He wore a jersey number 7 all his professional life that matched his 7 date of birth. His performance on the field was nothing short of magical. This is how lucky the number 7 is if it happens to be your number.

A new national hero was born in India in the month of November 2020. The managing partner of Republic Television (which he founded in 2017) and known for his aggressive style of anchoring and direct questioning, Mr. Arnab Goswami is an honest journalist and news anchor who ruffled the feathers of many corrupt politicians not used to truth-seeking news reporting. Mr. Arnab Goswami was arrested by the State Government of Maharashtra on a false case and tortured in custody just for being an honest reporter. Despite all the state government's attempts, the Supreme court of India granted him bail and ruled in the favor of personal liberty (a right of all Indian citizens that has been denied to them for many years). The entire country roared at his release. A rising political future for sure awaits Mr. Arnab Goswami, whose numbers merit a breakdown.

A R N A B   G O S W A M I
1+2+5+1+2   3+7+3+6+1+4+1
11   +   25   =36

Date of Birth: March 7, 1973
3+7+20   =30

Arnab Goswami has some very powerful numbers. Being a Pisces, he is ruled by the largest planet Jupiter which is represented by the number 3. His compound number further expands on the energy of planet Jupiter, adding up to a number 30. On his birthday in 2020, he entered his 48th year of life, further amplifying the energy of planet Jupiter that aligns him with lifetime fame and success.

His popular name has the energy of number 11, a master number, and number 25, a very intuitive energy that works with his date of birth. The name number 36 is a number of success to any enterprise and also makes him bold, strong, and aggressive in his speech.

M U M B A I
4+6+4+2+1+1   =18

The number 18 that represents the city of Mumbai does not work for Arnab Goswami. He needs to be cautious with his own personal safety while living in this city.

People born with the energy of number 7 are highly intuitive and should always work with their intuition and never second guess themselves; their gut feeling is invariably right.

CHAPTER TWELVE

NUMBER

8

The mighty number 8 is a very powerful number. In Far East countries like China and other Pacific rim countries, the number 8 is used extensively. People living in that part of the world believe the pronunciation of number 8 carries positive energies and they use 8 in their car license plates, telephone numbers, home addresses, businesses, and just about everywhere possible.

Vedic tradition, however, has a different perspective of number 8. According to astronumerology, the number 8 is represented by planet Saturn. This planet is known as a hard task master. The analogy is that Saturn is like a strict schoolteacher conducting a class with a cane in his hand. Saturn demands order, discipline, organization, and for things to be done in an orderly fashion.

At the same time, when the system is followed correctly, Saturn rewards you wonderfully.

I've met many clients over the years who were born on dates of birth ruled by Saturn. They all had difficult lives in their early years. Most of them who got married in their early 20s experienced challenging relationships and either separated or divorced. One couple that stands out is a young lady and her husband who consulted with me for a number of years. Both husband and wife had Saturn dates of birth and both were born under the sign Scorpio. I remember working with them to resolve a complex legal matter regarding a business they owned and by the grace of God, they prevailed. They had a horrible personal life, constantly bickering while raising their two autistic sons. The husband befriended another woman who became the mother of his daughter and the wife was busy on her dating circuit. They are separated now. This example serves to demonstrate what happens when two number 8 people marry early in life. If you happen to carry this energy, please be cautious when it comes to getting into a relationship. Based on my experience with this number, marriage works better after the age of 28. Former First Lady Hillary Clinton is also born on a Saturn date of birth under the sign Scorpio. This number is also responsible for depression. The energy intensifies when a person with this energy enters a personal year 4 or 8.

During the earlier part of the year, Sun signs like Capricorn and Aquarius carry the energy of planet Saturn during the colder months. The month of October also carries the energies of planet Saturn.

Shades of number 8—like 17, 26, 35, 44, 53, and so on—carry the energy of this planet. It is also believed that the number 8 is the sign of infinity and people born under this sign find it hard to overcome many life challenges if their energies are not balanced properly.

Dharmendra is a famous Bollywood actor. He has a Saturn date of birth and got married when he was quite young. As his career progressed, he got married to Hema Malini, one of his film costars, with whom he had two daughters. He too had an early marriage because of his Saturn date of birth.

Numbers that work well with the energy of number 8 are 5, 6, and 3 with some exceptions. The number 15 does not work well with the number 8 and should be avoided.

Numbers that don't work well with the number 8 are 4, 8, 9, 2, and 7. Number 1 is a neutral vibration for this number. I had a client some years ago who lived in a home number 489 in California's Central Valley. He told me that he didn't feel fulfilled, so I suggested he change his residence and he agreed. Since moving, things have improved for him and his family and he feels happier.

All name vibrations in personal or business use need to be balanced with the positive numbers indicated earlier. Colors like blue, beige, and green work well for this energy and darker colors like black, red, and brown should be avoided at all times. These lighter colors can be used in garments, cars, or other places as needed.

If applied correctly, this information will help those with Saturn vibrations overcome their challenges and transition through changes more smoothly. If a person with Saturn energy doesn't employ the right knowledge, he or she will keep bumping heads from the beginning until the end and won't understand why.

The gemstone that best suits the number 8 is emerald. One personality often seen wearing an emerald ring to balance the energy of planet Saturn is Mr. Amitabh Bachchan. This gemstone has worked wonderfully for him and promoted him to become the most sought-after actor in the Indian film industry. Emerald is worn in a ring on the small finger or as a pendant to activate the heart chakra. It opens the heart chakra for unconditional love and manifestation and to attract wealth. Famous celebrities wear emerald for luck and prosperity because it represents the energy of number 5.

The numbers 4 and 8 pull each other magnetically but then start spiraling downwards. Number 4 is associated with the planet Uranus and number 8 with the planet Saturn. Number 4 is fast-moving and unconventional while number 8 is slow, strict, and disciplined. I've realized over the years that whenever these two numbers come together—in a date of birth, personal name, business, or address—they attract more of the same energy. This combination creates challenging energies. It's like stepping into quicksand you can't get out of.

I've met people who write down a number 8 on a piece of paper and keep it in their pockets, purses, or wallets for success. The number 8 is a sign of infinity but keeping it inside a place of money doesn't work to actually attract money. On the contrary, it can actually block one's luck. The energy of this number is very restrictive and there are many other lucky number combinations that can be used based on our basic energy. Always consider which numbers are luckiest for you by evaluating the numbers in your date of birth. A couple who relocated from France to Miami used to do this exact thing. The husband couldn't close any real estate deals and the wife's creative business wasn't doing well either. The energy shifted once the number 8 was removed from their wallets and their business energies were free to flow once more.

Here's one example of how the combination of 4 and 8 work together:

$$S \quad O \quad L \quad Y \quad N \quad D \quad R \quad A$$
$$3+7+3+1+5+4+2+1 \qquad =26$$

During the presidency of Barack Obama, the White House opened a company called Solyndra that made national news in the city of Fremont, California. This company was created as a clean tech company that would manufacture solar panels. If you look at the name Solyndra, it carries the number 26, the vibration of planet Saturn, and it also has eight letters in its name. The name vibration of the city of Fremont also carries the Saturn vibration. The federal government invested 535 million dollars, and here comes the energy of Uranus. Solyndra was operating in four buildings, another Uranus number 4. President Obama visited this company on May 26, 2011 and the Uranus and Saturn vibrations appear again. It was on August 31, 2011 that this company filed for bankruptcy and shut its doors. It was on September 8, 2011 that an investigation into this company began. President Biden, who was Vice President when Solyndra went bankrupt, restarted the loan program that backed Solyndra in March 2021. This is not a good idea.

We all understand that to run a successful business, one needs a solid plan, intelligent, hard-working people, and money to make the business function smoothly. But another often over-looked aspect that must be considered is the angle of numerology. The numbers 4 and 8 will attract one another but then sink the best efforts, even if these efforts are funded by the highest sources.

Imran Khan is the current Prime Minister of Pakistan and its 22nd Prime Minister. He was born on October 5, 1952 and is also the former cricket captain of Pakistan that won the world cup in 1992. Very charismatic and successful in his younger days, Mr. Khan also realized his dream to become the top official of his country.

$$I\ M\ R\ A\ N \qquad\qquad K\ H\ A\ N$$
$$1+4+2+1+5 \qquad\qquad 2+5+1+5$$
$$13 \qquad + \qquad 13 \qquad\qquad =26$$

$$\text{Date of Birth: October 5, 1952}$$
$$10+5+17 \qquad\qquad =32$$

This number pattern is rare. Number 13 repeating twice and adding up to a 26 is a difficult combination. It brings challenges in partnerships and relationships and the person has to be giving at all times in order to be successful. Mr. Khan did give back to the community by creating a cancer hospital dedicated to his mother. Born as a Libra, he's under the influence of planets Venus and Saturn, the hard task master. Mercury supports him by making him an eloquent speaker and blesses him with intelligence to accomplish his personal ambitions. Unfortunately, the year 2021 doesn't complement the energy of Pakistan. Mr. Khan should be careful of his position that could be taken away and throw him into a state of extreme depression.

Deep and spiritual, number 8 people work for others, generate money for others, and help family members young and old. They diligently work to the top and are always fair and balanced in their approach. They should avoid the legal system and any form of trickery or manipulation. The terrorist attacks in Paris happened on November 13, 2015, which again illustrates the mysterious attraction of numbers 4 and 8 towards one another.

Number 8 people will benefit most from the real estate business. They should work with properties and land to benefit in their lives. Because they are represented by planet Saturn, they often inherit properties from their parents or ancestors. They should never start a new project on a 4, 8, or any of their combinations. Partnership in business is also not a good idea and they should also avoid driving cars that are black or red. I know number 8 people who are very successful in real estate and make money but still feel depressed. They often have challenging marriages and separate from their spouses at a later stage in life but still support them monetarily. They like to be close to their families and have no problem helping them financially whenever needed. They carry pains of separation or from rough childhoods and often spoil their children by over caring for them. Alcohol and substance abuse is also common in number 8 people. They should be very careful making new friends, as they're easily tricked and taken advantage of.

From my experience, number 8 benefits from donating to the needy on Saturday, a day that's ruled by the energy of planet Saturn per Vedic traditions. Giving money, food, or clothing to the needy on this day will return as new blessings in their lives. Number 8 people should make this a regular practice in their lives.

Number 17

Number 17 carries the energies of number 1 and 7 and, both being compatible, work magically
to attract fame and success.

People with this date of birth have to work for the dollar from a young age. Their personal relationships work better after the age of thirty and they should avoid business partnerships, as they work better on their own. They naturally attract fame and success in their lives.

Famous personalities who were born on the 17th are the Former First Lady of the United States Michelle Obama and the Prime Minister of India Mr. Narendra Modi. The famous NBA basketball player Michael Jordan also has this date of birth. The number 5 compliments this number well.

The world knows 9/11 and the events surrounding the World Trade Center in New York at the beginning of the 20th century. During this crisis, Rudy Giuliani was the 107th mayor in charge of New York City. Tragic as those events were, Mayor Rudy Giuliani handled the crisis well. It was the number 107 that attracted him to give him fame that would be with him even after he leaves the earth.

So if number 17 happens to be in your space I have one piece of advice: Respect it.

G O L D
3+7+3+4   =17

We all know the value of gold. Many traditions around the world use gold and regard it as a very precious metal. Gold represents the planet Jupiter, the largest planet, and those who have a weak Jupiter energy in their charts are advised to wear gold. However, it is important to know that gold does not work with everyone. I personally like the energy of gold as it works well for me.

The vibration of the word gold adds up to a number 17. The year 2021 adds up to a number 5, which works well with the energy of gold. This is why the price of gold will continue to rise as 2021 progresses.

CHAPTER THIRTEEN

NUMBER

9

The mighty number 9 is a powerful number represented by planet Mars and associated with energy, fire, and aggression. This number is also called the cosmic firecracker because if there is no energy, nothing can move on Earth.

Number 9 works well with the energy of number 6, associated with the planet Venus, and number 3, associated with the planet Jupiter. Conversely, numbers 5, 4, and 8 do not work well with this number. Please avoid these numbers if you are a number 9.

Number 9 can appear in our dates of birth, street addresses, businesses, cars, telephone numbers, and many other places. I would like to give you examples of both sides of Mars' energy.

I consulted with a client who lives the in San Francisco Bay Area for many years. She works at a prestigious hospital for a number of years. She came to consult with me during a very diffi-cult time of her life after her young son became a victim of gang violence. The family was shattered emotionally and were trying to heal from the pain, as anyone else in that position would. She was born under the sign Virgo and ruled by the energy of planet Mercury. Her home, however, carried intense Mars energy that helped her get a job at the hospital but that was destructive to the wellbeing of the family. She agreed to patch her house to shift the energy to a vibration that would work with other family members. At the time, her relationship with her husband was also not the best and her other two grown-up children were struggling in their relationships, too. A few months after the house was patched, the vibration shifted to benefit the other family members and things started slowly falling in place. Her daughter got happily mar-ried and her son was employed in the same medical facility as his mother. My client had a habit of having to consult different people at all times and creating challenges for herself even after she had found peace in her house. I wish she would have more faith in God and become more spiritual in the sense of listening to her own intuition when she saw that things were improving. As we can see from this example, the energy of number 9 when it's a number in a home address can be very difficult number to handle, especially if this number does not suit you. Using more of the color red inside the home or in the landscape outside is not recommended, as red is associated with fire and intensity. I have seen many celebrities with the energy of Mars in their names that brought them huge financial success and fame. This energy works well with real estate business names and addresses.

Those who live in the United States know that retailers often prefer to make the prices of items they sell end in 99. For example, $5.99 or $689.99. The 99 cents that is added to selling prices represents the energy of Mars twice and that is pure energy. This energy moves items off the shelf and maintains the selling dynamic. It's one of the things that keeps our economy moving.

When the number 6 repeats three times, it adds up to a cer-tain kind of Mars energy. This combination is also mentioned in the Holy Bible (referred to as the "The Number of the Beast") and is not considered to be a very positive vibration. In fact, in the United States the Social Security Administration has discontinued the issuance of Social Security numbers that have the number 6 repeating three times for reasons best known to them.

Another example refers to an agency in the US called the INS. The world knows it as the powerful Immigration and Naturalization Service. The shortened and more popular name, INS, carries a Mars energy. Over the years, I have seen many immigrants who came to America and adjusted easily to pursue their American dream, but many others who were shown the door. It becomes evident that Mars works for some but not for all. If one has a lot of challenges, marital discord, injuries, accidents, or hospital visits, then the energy of Mars needs to be strengthened for that individual.

Number 9 carries the energy of the hot planet Mars and is an excellent number for companies that are in the telecommunications business. The president of the Reliance Group, Mukesh Ambani, owns a telecom company by the name of JIO. Mr. Ambani is one of the richest men on this planet and lives in South Mumbai in his two-billion-dollar tower called Antilia. The name JIO also carries the energy of Mars, the number 9, and it's well-known how successful Mr. Ambani's company has become in a short period of time. To make the energy of JIO even higher, the logo is red, which further amplifies Mars' energy. In early 2020, Mark Zuckerberg, the CEO of Facebook, invested over nine billion dollars in Mr. Ambani's new venture, JIO Reliance, enhancing the prospect of greater success to his company.

$$J \quad I \quad O$$
$$1+1+7 \quad =9$$

Another powerful mars energy is carried by Sonia Gandhi, the leader of the Congress Party in India. She is born on the 9th and her name vibration adds up to a profound Mars combination. Sonia Gandhi is worth billions of dollars, making her the fourth richest politician in the world.

This is another great example of the mighty energies of number 9.

The number 9 is ruled by planet Mars and is associated with speed and action. People who have this number in their charts are prone to accidents and should exercise caution around arms and ammunition. As a young officer in the Indian Army, I have had my fair share of this experience. Planet Mars, my ruler, certainly taught me few hard lessons when I was young and racing bikes. After maturing a little, I learned to wear White Pearl to calm my Mars energy and have used it ever since. I like to drive white colored cars as the vibration of this color keeps me calm and composed and grants me more control over my thoughts. If you have this energy, you can do what I did and you'll find it very helpful in the long run.

Slum Dog Millionaire is a popular film that was created in the slums of Mumbai, India. It showcased the poverty that exists in India and the will of the poor to survive and rise against all odds. The title of this film added a powerful Mars energy to it and for this reason, it ended up with many Oscars to its credit. This is a great example of the power packed-winning energy of planet Mars.

FedEx and Costco, two large US corporations, also boast the high energy of Mars:

F E D E X
8+5+4+5+5   =27

FedEx is a global company with a worldwide network. It has been successfully delivering for the last fifty years, even during the pandemic. The name of this company as indicated above combines to the overall energy of planet Mars that keeps it charged with movement at all times. The name also carries the number 5, the number of travel and communication, three times.

C O S T C O
3+7+3+4+3+7   =27

Costco is also a global company. Like FedEx, Costco also carries the energy of planet Mars and its success is unstoppable. The power of planet Mars supporting a business is a huge blessing.

Number 9 and My Life

Number 9 has been a big part of my life. Growing up in India, I was not aware of how numbers impact our lives. After I joined the Indian military academy, I started experiencing the energies of number 9. I remember firing on the rifle ranges with rifle number 27. My scores were always high but they curiously changed with each different rifle number. This made me think for a while but being fairly young at the time, it didn't make much sense to me. As time passed, I realized that my Mars energy had a direct relationship with the number 9. And as I grew older, I noticed that the number 9 kept repeating in my life. This made me understand how important the energies of this number were in my life. I attended flight school at Meacham field in Fort Worth, TX and in my first check ride to get my private pilot's license, my examiner made me do a crosswind landing on RWY 27. The landing was smooth and soon after, the examiner issued me with my first certificate. My first apartment after immigrating to America had the number 27 which opened many doors for me and later, my first residence that fell on my lap had the number 6300.

We all have our lucky numbers that are determined by our date of birth. We should be using our unique number patterns constantly to our benefit. The energy of number 9 works well with gold and gems like Ruby, Red Coral, and White Pearl. Because 9 is a hot number, the energy of White Pearl introduces calmness and reduces anger and anxiety in number 9 people. I have personally worked with Red Coral for many years. The placement of the planet Mars favorably is very important for leading a peaceful and healthy life. I have consulted many people who have being facing the wrath of planet Mars. Red Coral can make a marriage happier and bring more stability and financial strength to one's life. It can pull one out of a confused mindset and lower energies and deliver success and prosperity. Native Indian people know the power of Red Coral and use it in most of their jewelry with turquoise. Wearing a Red Coral with yellow Sapphire brings great luck in owning real estate. I have met celebrities who are very fond of wearing Red Coral in rings and necklaces.

The title of this book, *All About Numbers*, carries the energies of my ruling planet Mars.

CHAPTER FOURTEEN

THE MASTER NUMBERS: 11, 22, 33, AND 44

Master numbers have a profound influence on our lives. The numbers 11, 22, 33, 44 are considered master numbers.

The master number 11 has the energy of the Sun twice as the number 1 is represented by Sun. This number is considered lucky if it appears in your date of birth. It makes one able to think "outside the box." Many opportunities come to this number, as well as a fair share of personal challenges. This is not an ideal business number and people with this number should pursue their talents and creativity.

If number 11 appears on a home or business address, it must be balanced with Sun and Neptune energies, the numbers 1 and 7, respectively. If it's not balanced properly, it could affect the finances and personal energies. The energies of numbers 1 and

7 could come from the name vibrations of people who live in the house or, in many cases, the actual name of the house. On a license plate, it needs to balance with the color of the vehicle.

We all remember that it was Apollo 11 that first took humans to the Moon. The famous Amitabh Bachchan was born on the 11th day and he encompasses the qualities of number 11 well. Mr. Bachchan is an Indian film actor, television host, and former politician. He's regarded as one of the greatest and most influential actors in the history of Indian cinema. Number 11 attracts and works well with the number 10 as that combination creates the yin and yang energy. I have met many intuitives over the years who lived in 11 homes but didn't realize how to handle its energies and consequently struggled with money and relationships.

I have a client in Southern California who's an eye doctor. He got a hold of my book and requested me to look into his home energy. I happened to be in LA at the time, so we were able to meet in person. As I pulled up to his property, I saw the number 11 on his home and knew that money energy and relationships within this home both needed help. After walking around his home (which had been visited by other consultants before me), I suggested a few changes, including adding a tiny number 4 between the number 11, to which he agreed. During our meeting, there was another lady present who also called herself an intuitive, but I later found out that she was actually his mistress. I could see the sadness in the wife's face. Soon after my client implemented the changes in his address, there was a shift in the energy of the household and the wife got rid of the other woman. She called me later and stated that she felt relieved to have regained control of her house and family. This example teaches us not to jump to conclusions about the number 11. Just because it's a master number doesn't mean it works for everyone.

Number 22 is another master number. This number comprises the energy of Moon twice and is beneficial in a date of birth when balanced with the energy of Sun. It's drawn to number 8 but doesn't work well with number 6 energies. In a home address, this number creates miscommunication. People coming to this number house often get confused finding it. It would have to be patched to match the energies of all occupants of the house. The popular and longstanding car brand Honda has this energy on its name.

It is the last week of May in 2020 as I write this chapter and the havoc that 2020 has wreaked on planet Earth can be felt by every human being. The year 2020 contains two 0s, which amplify the energy of 22 in a big way. The energy of this year has turned everything upside down and we're all desperately trying to adjust to a new normal: social distancing, mandatory masks, remote learning, working from home, protests around the globe, and a struggling economy are just some of the ways in which our lives have transformed. The scores remain unsettled as countries come together to try and make things better. The year 2020 is an accurate, albeit unfortunate, example of the power of master number 22.

Master number 33 has the energy of Jupiter twice and is a great number. It works well if it resonates with your date of birth. I have personally experienced the energy of this number favorably. Many businesses that have been expanding and performing well have this number in their names. Many celebrities and famous faces have also used this number in their names to attain success.

In August 2010, 33 miners got stuck under the surface of the Earth for 69 days after an accident in the Copiapo minefields in Chile. The entire world witnessed how each one of the miners was pulled out in small capsules 2,300 feet under the surface of the Earth. I believe it was the number 33 that kept the energy high and hopeful and pulled everyone out safely. This is an inspirational example of the power of master number 33.

Master number 44 is a very interesting number. The very unconventional Uranus repeats twice on this number. Its energy was highlighted when former President Obama and then-Secretary of State Hillary Clinton were running to become the 44th president of the USA. Former President Obama prevailed because of the strong Sun energy in his chart. I would not, however, recommend this number on a residence or a business address. The number 44 carries the energy of unpredictable Uranus twice and adds up to a number 8 that brings in sinking energy. The numbers 4 and 8 should always be avoided as they tend to attract each other to create blocks and challenges.

11 11

I'm often asked by my clients about certain sets of numbers like 11 11, 12 12, or other such patterns that keep appearing in their lives or being shown to them by the universe.

Numbers are the language of the universe and the universe speaks to us through numbers. I believe strongly in the compatibility of numbers. If certain numbers appear in my life, the first thing I do is check if these numbers are compatible with mine.

If number 11 11 starts appearing in a person's life but it doesn't match that individual's date of birth, it would bring in relationship challenges and financial issues. If someone has the influence of numbers 1, 4, or 7 in their charts, then 11 11 means positive energies are flowing towards them. I had a client who would see the number 226 quite often. She had a 25 in her birthdate and I confirmed to her that each time she saw 226, good vibrations would flow towards her. Compatible numbers help us experience sudden improvements in luck and endow us with a higher sense of intuition. Before you decide to decode numbers that you're seeing constantly, check if they match your numeric energy. If not, be cautious of them.

I come across many people who choose master numbers in their homes, businesses, license plates, phone numbers, bank accounts etc. Most of them don't realize that master numbers have a very powerful energy and can be difficult to handle if they don't connect with their date of birth. Many people are often advised by their intuitives to use master numbers, without understanding how overwhelming or complex they can be. Please be wise before considering the use of master numbers and compare them first against your own number energies.

CHAPTER FIFTEEN

FINAL THOUGHTS ON NUMBERS

Some Other Thoughts

I have come across many clients who are unable to buy a home and even if they do, for some reason are unable to stay in their new home and end up as tenants again. One of the reasons is their connection with the energy of planet Earth. There are two gemstones that connect with the root chakra that I believe can strengthen our connection with Mother Earth: red coral and cat's eye. Red coral works with the numbers 3, 6, and 9 and cat's eye works with the numbers 1, 2, 4, and 7. They should be worn only after a person's chart is examined. If found suitable, these gemstones will help to open the root chakra and connection to the Earth.

Rudraksha beads are also used for the same purpose. I recommend wearing a 14 and 18 faceted rudraksha bead to open the root chakra and benefit from the Earth's energy and attract more wealth as well. If you want to own and live in your own home you should definitely consider these options.

- **Mission Name:** Mars 2020
- **Rover Name:** <u>Perseverance</u>
- **Main Job:** Seek signs of ancient life and collect samples of rock and regolith (broken rock and soil) for possible return to Earth.
- **Launch:** July 30, 2020
- **Landing:** February 18, 2021
- **Landing Site:** Jezero Crater, Mars

P E R S E V E R A N C E
8+5+2+3+5+6+5+2+1+5+3+5   =50

As mentioned earlier, the year 2021 is a mercurial year and many ups and downs will be witnessed in this year. The number 5 works well with another number 5. The name Perseverance carries the energy of the number 5 and was able to make the Mars mission a success. Another example of Mercury's energy has been witnessed by the State of Texas in the United States.

T E X A S
4+5+5+1+3   =18

The number 5 and the number 9 cause devastation when they come together. The state of Texas experienced a devastating winter storm in early 2021 that caused widespread water disruption and damages that would take months to fix. This natural calamity affected some 8.6 million people.

The year 2021 equals a 5 (2+0+2+1 = 5). 8.6 million people affected by the winter storms equals a 5 (8 + 6 = 14 or 5). Texas carries the energy of number 9. If you have these numbers, please be cautious when your energy changes. The numbers 5 and 9 do not like to dance together.

Number 5 is an unstable number and works well in the winter season that is influenced by the energy of planet Saturn, the number 8. The energy of number 5 will stabilize in the second half of 2021, bringing many positive changes to the planet.

I have been blessed to meet and consult with many people over the years and there are some that stay in my mind. I remember this one East Indian lady who came to me seeking to know what the numbers said about her young son who was about to enter into matrimony. The bride-to-be had some interesting numbers in her chart. After a quick review, I told her that the numbers were not compatible and that it would be a good idea to call of the marriage.

This was clearly not what she wanted to hear. Visibly disturbed by my answer, she told me that her future daughter-in-law was the daughter of a very famous astrologer who practiced in the San Francisco Bay Area. If this was the case, then why did she want a second opinion? Was it her intuition that had bought her to me? The marriage happened anyway.

After a few years, a mutual friend told me that the woman's son, the son-in-law of the famous astrologer, committed suicide. I also learned that the astrologer stopped consulting people after his own daughter became a widow. This made me very sad to hear, but reaffirmed my faith in the power of numbers.

Many people wear their lucky number as pendants or sometimes on bracelets. I have known people who write certain numbers on the palms of their hands each morning before starting the day. They believe this helps them align with the right energy for the day and keep luck on their side. I have also seen people write the number 8 on a piece of paper and keep it in their wallets or handbags, thinking that it's a symbol of infinity that will increase the flow of money. However, I would caution you against doing this as it can actually block the flow of money if the number 8 is not your energy. Virgos and Geminis ruled by the number 5 would be more successful in doing so, as both 5 and 8 compliment each other.

I have consulted with many well-adjusted people over the years who have tasted success. As we all know, time and money have to be respected and just like a wheel of fortune, life and circumstances can change for all of us. One such client of mine who had it all went off track with her personal relationships and things changed for her very quickly. Calling and consulting after the fact is a waste of time and money. Please use your common sense. Being grateful for what is given to us at all times is a good idea.

Client Experiences

The following are client experiences in their own words.

Many years ago, I met a client whose name was Mary. She had heard me on a local radio station in San Francisco and connected with me for a reading. Satisfied with my consultation, she referred me to her sister Sally who lived in the Monterey Peninsula in central California and who has been my client ever since. Some years later, Mary passed away battling breast cancer. Sally's experience and the reason she was directed to consult with me has been documented in her own words below.

I was quite taken aback after Sally narrated her experience with the intuitive mediator. It made me believe that I was on the right path and the information that was coming from me was true to be confirmed by the other side.

The Story of Sally C.

To experience the sudden loss of a loved one was emotionally overwhelming. In 2011, the tragedy of losing my sister without any warning was real. While grieving her loss, my husband and I were also enduring a critical financial crisis with our real estate. In a desperate attempt, I sought the advice of an intuitive mediator with the other side in hopes of connecting and finding answers to my sister's death. During my session, my sister's soul came though vividly in efforts to console my grief and help me through my current financial crisis. The intuitive stated that my sister wanted me to know her soul lives on but that I urgently needed to seek the advice of her previous business consultant, Jesse Kalsi, regarding my real estate crisis.

The days that followed were nothing short of miraculous. Once I contacted Jesse Kalsi, he reviewed the numerology on all 3 properties and gave me very specific and detailed steps on what to do in getting these properties sold with a quick escrow. Jesse stated that within a week, I would be contacted by the current mortgage company with a significant offer to sell. The following day, I found a certified letter from the bank with a $30,000 offer to sell my home within a 6-month period. Since this time, I have sought Jesse's advice on numerous high-income value properties with great success. I have the utmost respect and deep gratitude for Jesse's work. His gift is immeasurable in transforming my life.

The Story of Mohini and Anisha

Another client story I want to share is that of a mother and daughter of East Indian descent who came to consult with me some years ago. The mother, Mohini, was an architect by profession and worked for a prestigious company in the San Francisco Bay Area. Her older son who was soon to graduate from medical school was not present at the time. Her husband was also an engineer and gainfully employed. It is May 2020 as I write this page. The reason the mother came to see me was her daughter, Anisha, who accompanied her for the consultation. After looking at Anisha's numbers, I told them about some very contradicting numbers in the young girl's code and I suggested that she wear an emerald in a pendant to balance her heart chakra. The mother then confessed to me what was really bothering her. Her daughter's close friend had jumped off the Golden Gate Bridge and her daughter now wanted to follow her and do the same. She strongly felt that by following her friend she would be reunited with her. I consoled the young girl and reminded her how much her life was worth. I felt that she was fine as they left my office to get the pendant that I had suggested.

A couple of weeks later, Mohini called me in a disturbed state. She had received a call from the law enforcement telling her that her daughter had been saved by the Golden Gate Bridge Security staff as she attempted to jump off the bridge. I instantly felt that the pendant she wore after she met with me had saved her life. I met the mother some months later at a temple during a religious service. She was happy to report that her daughter had finally graduated and was working as a swim instructor for autistic kids. She was well and healed. Thank you God.

The Story of Melissa M.

I heard Jesse Kalsi do readings on the radio many times over the past 20 years. When I moved to San Francisco, 15 years ago, I finally decided to get a reading with him. I found his work fascinating and on his advice, moved to Noe Valley!

Fast forward four years later, I felt a strong urgency to move back to the coast to be close to the water for healing purposes. Well, I was so excited to find a one-bedroom apartment right on the waterfront. Although the rent was challenging, I didn't care, because I just had to be as close to the ocean as possible.

My new apartment was beautiful, however, I could not sleep in my bedroom due to the "bad vibes" I could feel in the air. So I set up a floor bed with blankets near the sliding glass door to be close to the water, that was right off the balcony.

I put a call in to my trusted Feng Shui Lady, knowing she could remedy the situation. Sure enough, she validated my intuition and assessed my bedroom as very dark, negative energy. Her expert advice was to get Earth energy into the bedroom as soon as possible.

I took her advice right away and purchased a big poster of tall trees with a dirt road going down the middle of them. The trees had lots and lots of moss hanging off the branches that I found quite healing and breathtaking. I had the poster professionally framed and hung it in my bedroom, in hopes of a brighter day.

In the interim, I was taking a manifestation six-week meditation class. Every time we meditated in class, a vision of a white horse came to me. *White horse*, I thought, *Why a white horse?* I had been taking meditation classes for the past 20 years and almost never had a vision come to me during meditation, nor did I have an affinity for white horses. *Strange*, I thought, and yet I could not figure out what the white horse meant. I was baffled.

One morning, one of my best friends called and asked me if I was interested in renting a studio apartment in the back of a house in Montara for $700. Her friend was listing this house and wanted to know if I was interested. I picked up the key that morning and reluctantly drove to Montara. The street was difficult to find and after a half an hour of being lost, I finally found the street in the back of the valley.

As I turned onto this street, a half block up, I spotted a small horse ranch. To my great surprise, as I got closer, there was a white horse hanging his head over the fence and staring straight at me as I turned onto the street. *Oh my God*, I thought, *it's the White Horse!*

I finally approached the house rental at the end of the dirt road, and excitedly got out to walk down the stairs to the studio apartment. I spent two hours on the property, contemplating, *This is a no brainer, Melissa*. However, I was torn because I had just found the apartment of my dreams on the water. I had only been there for three months—how could I give it up now?

Deep in contemplation, I found myself staring out of one of the windows of the apartment. The view was of only tall trees with moss hanging off them, just like in my poster. My jaw dropped in amazement.

On top of that, a few minutes later I realized I had a dream of my best pal's friend, who was the listing agent of this house. In this dream, I climbed in the window of a house to speak with her urgently. The dream was so strong that I called my friend the next day to make sure she was ok. They were offering this apartment to me before it was even put on the market, I had to give them an answer that evening.

Three signs, I thought to myself, *what more do you need?* I felt perplexed and before leaving the apartment, I suddenly remembered Jesse Kalsi. *I have to call him*, I thought, *but how am I going to reach him today?* I also didn't have the money for the reading, as my current oceanfront rent was so expensive. I reminded myself that this was an important life decision, so I spent the last money I had in hopes of the highest outcome of my future.

I picked up the phone and to my surprise, Jesse answered right away. I told him I urgently needed a reading and his response was, "I can give you a reading, but it has to be now." I was truly amazed and grateful and told him my birth information for the reading. I gave him the Montara address first and he responded, "This place is very, very good for you." I proceeded to give him the address of the oceanfront apartment, and he immediately exclaimed with conviction, "Destruction. You need to leave this property as soon as possible." Surprised, I asked, "What do you mean by destruction?" Jesse replied, "It's bad for your health, work, and relationships and you were guided to contact me. We continued with a one hour reading and he continued to reiterate how important it was for me to vacate the oceanfront apartment as soon as possible.

As we were talking, my black cat, out of character, proceeded to crawl up my leg. As I was shooing him down, Jesse asked, "Who is that?" "That's my cat, Magic," I responded.

Jesse then said, "Your cat is very psychic and so are you. You both vibrate at the same frequency. Your cat has been trying to tell you that you have to leave." I told Jesse that my cat had been scratching the front door in the middle of the night for the past two weeks as well as going to the bathroom outside of the litter box, neither of which he had ever done in the past.

After we hung up the phone, I immediately called the listing agent and took the Montara rental. I gave *one* month's notice to my current landlord and from that night on, my cat never scratched the front door or went to the bathroom outside of the litter box again.

One month after I moved out of the oceanfront apartment, the entire building was red-tagged and evacuated, as it was starting to slip into the ocean. Not long after, the apartments were torn down. From that day on, I promised to myself to consult Jesse first before moving anywhere!

Made in the USA
Las Vegas, NV
11 September 2021